BECOMING A LEADER OF CHARACTER

"My father, who retired as an Admiral in the US Navy, taught me that great leaders are great because their people trust and respect them—not because they have power. Father and son Gen. James L. Anderson, USA (Ret.) and Dave Anderson drill that message home in *Becoming a Leader of Character*. Leaders of character know true leadership is not about them; it's about the people they serve. The world is in desperate need of a different leadership role model—and this book is a powerful guide for leaders who strive toward that goal."

– **Ken Blanchard**, coauthor of
The New One Minute Manager® and *Leading at a Higher Level*

"This magnificent book is a superb mix of behavioral science, philosophy and common sense. The multi-generational counterpoint writing style is laden with real-life stories that are relatable to today's fast-paced workplace environment. Because of the authors' thoughtful analysis, this book contains many leadership ideas worthy of introspection. As a former CEO of several companies and Chairman of a Fortune 200 company, I highly recommend it to all who are interested in leading others in the 21st century."

– **Lieutenant General USA Retired John Moellering**,
Chairman Emeritus, USAA

"In business and in the military, *Courage, Humility, Integrity, Selflessness, Duty* and *Positivity* are the key character habits a leader must display. *Becoming a Leader of Character* is an uncomplicated approach to developing a leader's most important leadership tool—character."

– **Joe DePinto**, President and CEO, 7-Eleven Inc.

"As Jim and Dave Anderson say, "Don't just read this book. Use it!" A father/son team of West Point graduates talking about leadership and character is what first got my interest. But then, it was their approach to developing character that hooked me. This is not the first book I have read that says a leader's character is important. But it is the first book I've read that provides specific steps that anyone can take to develop that character. There is something to learn in every chapter without sounding academic. The stories are engaging and honest, the definitions are simple and the solutions are accessible. This is truly a unique leadership book and a must read for a CEO or a brand new leader."

– **Bob Funk**, CEO, Express Employment Professionals

"When fresh voices put new perspective on something and still make it accessible to all of us, I stop and pay attention. General Jim Anderson and Dave Anderson have done just that. Not only do they have the credentials to speak to us about leadership, but the way they approach the issue of character is both inspiring and challenging all at the same time. Building character is an exercise that takes determination and consistent effort. But the returns for the leader and the led are immeasurable. Don't just read *Becoming a Leader of Character*, use it daily and prepare to grow as a leader!"

– **Karen Dillon**, former Editor of the *Harvard Business Review* and author of *New York Times* best-seller *How Will You Measure Your Life*

"Brigadier General (Retired) Jim Anderson and his son, Dave, have written the definitive book on leadership. This is a must read for every leader or aspiring leader regardless of age. It goes well beyond everyday theories and concepts and provides concrete examples of why and how to become a leader of character. As they say, you have to DO what you want to BE. If you want to continue to grow and develop into a great leader of character, this book is the perfect blueprint for you."

– **Lieutenant General Buster Hagenback**, USA Retired, Former Superintendent, United States Military Academy at West Point

"From ancient Greek philosophers to modern savants, history is replete with attempts to define character. Breaking away from the numbing array of authors dealing with character and leadership, the Andersons—father and son—not only define *what* character is and show *why* it is essential in leaders, they also describe *how* it is developed. Combining those three factors makes this volume a most significant contribution to the literature on leadership. Furthermore, and importantly, its down-to-earth prose and real-world context move it into the category of must-have books for anyone aspiring to lead."

– **Lieutenant General David Palmer**, USA Retired, former Superintendent, United States Military Academy at West Point

"The Anderson's have hit it out of the park with this book! Leadership is character in action which is simply doing the right thing - even when it costs you something - especially when it costs you something as I'm not sure it can be an act of character unless it costs you something. The key that most authors miss is that character is habit, repeated behavior over time. You don't develop humility or selflessness reading books or going to a seminar. These skills must be practiced! This great book gives you practical applications and exercises to get the principles into your game!"

— **Jim Hunter** bestselling author,
The Servant - A Simple Story About The True Essence of Leadership

"People often confuse 'leading' with a self-claimed title that boasts of being aggressive, direct and intelligent. In this book we are reminded that noble character emerges softly as confidence, humility and integrity, thereby opening doors for true leadership. Whatever your position, you can learn these habits and develop a team, a family and a community of character and influence."

— **Dan Miller**, *New York Times* bestselling author,
48 Days to the Work You Love

"From corporate boardrooms, to ball fields, to our nation's government and even in our homes we are in the midst of a leadership crisis. At the core of this crisis is the foundational element that leadership is built on, which is character. I can think of no father-and-son team better suited to address this and offer up pragmatic solutions than my friend Dave Anderson and his father General Jim Anderson. This is a must read for every business leader, coach, parent or leader of any kind. This influential book contains the power to change organizations and people's lives in a very profound way, and I know that my copy will be dog eared, highlighted and quoted often."

— **Scott MacGregor**, Founder and President of Something New

"Wow! What a book — in fact, THE book that should be on every modern leader's desk. The formula for becoming and being a great leader is in these pages. If you are new to leadership *Becoming a Leader of Character* will give you the tools you need to get people to follow you. If you've been leading people for a while I promise you'll be writing in the margins and highlighting pages as you reflect on the habits you need to change."

— **Jeb Blount**, author of *People Follow You:
The Real Secret to What Matters Most in Leadership*

"My experience at West Point was a transformational one that prepared me to lead wherever I was serving—be it on the battlefield in the military, or in the boardroom in corporate America. *Becoming a Leader of Character* captures the true essence of what it takes to be a successful leader at any level ... character. Equally important, it illustrates a road map to building the character and leadership traits essential to becoming a leader worth following. Do these exercises and you will be following a plan that will impact your work teams and your family because they will see you as a *Leader of Character* and want to follow you. People follow character!"

– **Daren Rebelez**, CEO of IHOP, International House of Pancakes

"When you are ready to Lead Positive—think like a leader, relate like a leader, engage like a leader, act like a leader, and serve like a leader—read this book. It will transform your life and work!"

– **Dr. Joey Faucette**, #1 bestselling author of *Work Positive in a Negative World*

"Do you have a plan—not just a desire—to build your character? Leaders work hard to improve their intellect and acquire technical skills. How many have a systematic plan to build that cornerstone of leadership—character? Jim and Dave Anderson have created a unique tool that is perfectly suited to help you do just that."

– **David Kim**, Partner, Apax Partners and President of Children of Fallen Patriots Foundation

"Justice Scalia once said, 'Bear in mind that brains and learning, like muscle and physical skill, are articles of commerce. They are bought and sold. You can hire them by the year or by the hour. The only thing in the world not for sale is character.' Though you can't buy character, West Point has proven you can develop it. Buy this book and let two of West Point's distinguished graduates lead you through the process."

– **Bob Eisiminger**, President and CEO, Knight Point Systems and Chairman of the Board, Wounded Warrior Amputee Softball Team

"If you are leading a multi-million dollar company, a local business, or a family, *Becoming a Leader of Character* tells us how to develop the *Courage*,

Humility, Integrity, Selflessness, Duty and *Positivity* that we all need to practice and pass on to those we lead. This book is easy to read and applies to all of us. It should be a textbook in businesses, in schools and in our homes that we all implement and learn from."

— **Matt Moellering**, COO Express Inc. and L.L. Bean Board Member.

"General Jim's observations on leading with character – and his personal stories of being such a leader – are so powerful and impactful. What draws me to General Jim's talks is that he is able to use very simple concepts to make a *profound* emotional impact on his listeners that change their lives. I could not be more pleased that readers across the world will now have that same opportunity. This is a book every leader and aspiring leader should read!"

— **Steven B. Wiley** President,
The Lincoln Leadership Institute at Gettysburg

"This father-son book by Dave and General Anderson speaks from their hearts about their passion—Leadership and Character. It will resonate with those that are willing to commit themselves to become leaders based on developing *Habits of Character* in order to become a *Leader of Character*. It applies to emerging leaders and those willing to dedicate themselves on building a true foundation to lead. Join their passion!"

— **Tim Issaco**, COO Orion International

"Dave and 'The General' hit the nail on the head when it comes to identifying today's leadership challenges. What we do is a direct reflection of who we are, and in today's fast-paced world, personal values often times get lost in the chaos of the day. *Becoming A Leader Of Character* offers practical exercises for strengthening our values and becoming the leader we all want to be. This is a must read for not just every 'leader,' but every person."

— **Jeff Boss**, Founder, Tier One Leadership Solutions, author of *Navigating Chaos: How To Find Certainty In Uncertain Situations*, former Navy SEAL

"The time has finally come for the General and his son, David to put pen to paper and create a marvelous and intriguing look at the journey of *Becoming a Leader of Character*. Over the past two decades, while at two separate Fortune 500 companies, I have seen the life changing impact the Andersons' principles of leadership character have had on countless leaders at all levels of an organization. The impact is real and lasting."

— **Frederick E Lord**, IV President, BlueC

"Years ago a friend pointed out to me that the root word for inheritance not only means a gift but the deeper meaning is literally an assignment and a task. It is that deeper meaning that is so evident in this book. What has been passed from father to son is not just lessons and examples but an assignment - the assignment of leadership. If you want to leave the best kind of inheritance to your own children please leave them the task and the expectation of leadership. But give them the preparation for that inheritance this book provides."

— **Fred Smith**, President, The Gathering

"People don't quit companies. They quit their managers. *Becoming a Leader of Character* is chock-full of ideas that managers, of any level, can use to up their game."

— **Lee Salz**, bestselling author of *Hire Right, Higher Profits*

BECOMING
— A —
LEADER
— OF —
CHARACTER

6 Habits that Make or Break
a Leader at Work and at Home

GEN. JAMES L. ANDERSON, USA (RET.)
AND DAVE ANDERSON

New York

BECOMING A LEADER OF CHARACTER
6 Habits that Make or Break a Leader at Work and at Home

Published in New York, New York, by Morgan James Publishing. Morgan James and The Entrepreneurial Publisher are trademarks of Morgan James, LLC. www.MorganJamesPublishing.com

The Morgan James Speakers Group can bring authors to your live event. For more information or to book an event visit The Morgan James Speakers Group at www.TheMorganJamesSpeakersGroup.com.

Shelfie

A free eBook edition is available
with the purchase of this print book.

CLEARLY PRINT YOUR NAME ABOVE IN UPPER CASE

Instructions to claim your free eBook edition:
1. Download the Shelfie app for Android or iOS
2. Write your name in **UPPER CASE** above
3. Use the Shelfie app to submit a photo
4. Download your eBook to any device

ISBN 978-1-63047-937-4 paperback
ISBN 978-1-63047-938-1 eBook
ISBN 978-1-63047-939-8 hardcover
Library of Congress Control Number:
2016900249

Cover Design by:
Chris Treccani
www.3dogdesign.net

In an effort to support local communities and raise awareness and funds, Morgan James Publishing donates a percentage of all book sales for the life of each book to Habitat for Humanity Peninsula and Greater Williamsburg.

Get involved today, visit
www.MorganJamesBuilds.com

Habitat
for Humanity®
Peninsula and
Greater Williamsburg
Building Partner

From General James L. Anderson

To my wife of sixty years, Joyce. She has been the bedrock of our family. She traveled the world with me in the Army for forty-two years and has contributed the central focus in raising our children, Terri Lynn Hover and David Anderson.

From Dave Anderson

For my family, Elizabeth, Samantha, and Jake. My wife Elizabeth, the model of *Integrity* in our family, who continues to love me even when I do not always live up to the principles in this book. My daughter Samantha who so often sets an example for her dad in *Humility, Selflessness, and Duty.* My son Jake who continues to impress me with his *Courage, Selflessness, and Positivity.* I am a blessed man.

We both dedicate this book to the men and women in the armed forces who have stepped forward and said, "Send me!" We were honored to serve with many of you and continue to be humbled by all your sacrifices on behalf of our country.

CONTENTS

FOREWORD

By Mike Krzyzewski
Duke University Basketball Coach
5-Time NCAA Basketball Champion
2-Time Olympic Gold Medal Head Coach
#1 All-Time Coaching Career Victories in NCAA Men's Basketball

"You have to DO what you want to BE." You will see this quote in the early pages of this book. If you want to BE a great leader, a *Leader of Character*, you have to DO what great leaders do. Just like good basketball players practice in order to become great basketball players, good leaders must practice in order to become great leaders.

Character is what separates great leaders—whether in sports, business, or any other vocation—from the rest of the pack. Our character is in our own control. We build it, sustain it, or destroy it based on our choices. The choices we make daily prepare us for the bigger choices that will come when challenges arise. Those daily choices are the practice drills that form our *Habits of Character*.

Why You Should Listen to These Guys

I do not know of another father-and-son team better suited to provide us with the why, what, and how of becoming a *Leader of Character* than Jim Anderson and his son Dave. These two generations of West Point graduates wrote a book that is straightforward, practical, and accessible, much like the authors are. Whether you are a CEO or a recent high school graduate, the Andersons speak with clarity to all leaders.

Yes, the Andersons and I attended the same school, West Point, albeit in three different decades. And yes, our beliefs on leadership run in parallel because of that common background. But my belief in them runs deeper than graduating from the same great leadership university.

I first met Major Jim Anderson almost fifty years ago when I was a young cadet at West Point in the late 1960s. He was there to train me and other cadets to become *Leaders of Character*. He was a firm, confident, and humble leader. He modeled everything right and true about leadership for everyone he encountered. He left a lasting impression on me as a young leader.

A decade later after a phone call from another mentor of mine, Coach Bob Knight, then Colonel Jim Anderson went from being my boxing instructor to my advocate. When my alma mater debated whether to bring in a new, untested coach, with an unpronounceable last name, to lead West Point's basketball team, I had a well-respected leader in my corner. Colonel Anderson prevailed, and I had my first head coaching job.

During my five years coaching at West Point, a lot of great leaders impacted my philosophy on leadership. But I could always look to Jim Anderson as a model of what I needed to DO in order for me to BE the *Leader of Character* I wanted to become.

It was also during those years that I first met Dave Anderson. I would see him sitting with his father at almost every home basketball game and during many of our practices in the West Point Field House. Dave was also one of the campers to sign up for my first ever basketball camp as a college head coach.

I remember that Dave was not a particularly gifted player during his summers attending our camp but that did not stop him. I saw the desire and the effort that told me he was Jim Anderson's son. His record in leading in both the Army and corporate America confirmed that for me again. Today, it does not surprise me that Dave has devoted his life's work to developing *Leaders of Character* much like his father has.

Why You Should Read This Book

Whether it is Jim's battles in Southeast Asia, Dave's battles in the corporate world, or my own battles on the basketball courts of the NCAA tournaments or the Olympics, we all learned the same thing—character matters.

I have had the honor to coach many great young men during my over forty years as a head coach at West Point and at Duke University. When recruiting I always look for youngsters who not only have outstanding talent and academic ability but, even more importantly, have great character.

One of the best youngsters I ever recruited was Shane Battier. The character that he displayed over a four-year period for me was truly amazing. He served as an example on and off the court of how a Duke basketball player should play and act. As a result, he ended up being the winningest player in the history of the NCAA, with 133 wins to his credit. I never worried about the conduct of my team while Shane was the leader.

The Andersons begin with the idea that most leadership failures are character failures. Most leaders' failures are not the result of a lack of management skills (competence) but a failure in character. All the money we spend on training competencies has missed the mark, because we are not addressing the number one reason leaders fail—and that is character. That is why the Andersons have devoted this book and, in fact, their professional lives to developing *Leaders of Character*. They convincingly argue that the cause of most character failures comes from a place of fear or pride. *Courage* and *Humility* are not only the antidote to fear and pride. They are also essential *Habits of Character* anyone can develop.

In my book *Leading with the Heart*, I stated, "True bravery in leadership revolves around the degree to which a person maintains the courage of his convictions." A *Leader of Character* does not change his values because things become difficult.

Courage and *Humility* are the bedrock *Habits of Character* that make the other habits possible. *Integrity* is not possible without the *Courage* to stand alone. *Selflessness* is not possible without the *Humility* to put the needs of others before your own. The Andersons understand these moral facts.

What's Different Here?

When I coach the Duke players or the Olympic team during practice, we know that how we practice will determine how we play on game day. In the same way, how we live our lives—the daily choices we make in relation to our character—will determine how we respond when the big challenges come. So what are the character drills and the exercises a leader needs to do to become a *Leader of Character*? That is where this book differs from other books on leadership I have read. Jim Anderson (*The General*) and Dave Anderson (*The Business Guy*) don't just tell you how you should respond to the big challenges leaders face. They lay out specific exercises to practice in your daily life. They give you exercises to practice *Courage* and *Humility* and four other virtues. These small character choices prepare you before you are faced with bigger decisions. They are specific exercises you can DO so you can BE the *Leader of Character* needed in today's world.

I am a basketball coach. As a basketball coach, I will always be an advocate for practice. In order to accomplish hard things, a basketball player must be willing to sweat in practice so he can be great in games. As the Andersons point out, if you are not willing to put in the work and break a sweat to become a great leader, then this is not the book for you. But if you are willing to take on the challenge of becoming a *Leader of Character* through sweat and practice, Jim and Dave Anderson have laid out the workout plan that will get you there.

"You have to DO what you want to BE." Now it is time for you to make a choice. What is it going to be? Are you willing to DO the work to BE the *Leader of Character* you can become?

If I had a whistle right now, I'd blow it so we could start practice.

Chapter 1

LEADERSHIP: WHY WE MUST CHANGE THE FOCUS

Our Why

There is a crisis of leadership in the world today. That may not be news to you. All you have to do is read a newspaper, watch the nightly news, or scan the Internet to see that the lack of good leadership is one of the central problems in our world.

Yet, books on leadership abound. So why this book? Why another book on leadership? Our reason is this: the book you hold in your hands is a different type of leadership book. We have read many of the books that are out there on leadership and watched as the crisis in leadership in all parts of our culture has continued to grow. We realize that plenty of people are devoting themselves to stopping this deterioration in leadership. They have written books and produced leadership seminars, claiming to have the answers for changing leaders. These books and seminars cover management techniques, personality traits, building trust, building teams, and improving coaching for performance. These approaches are not bad, but we believe they miss the root cause of the issue. We believe that the majority of the leadership offerings available are treating the symptoms of the leadership crisis and not the underlying disease. Our book is here to help all of us who are motivated and ready to treat that disease.

We Have a Sick Patient—and the Patient Is Not Getting Better

Most of the leadership books and seminars available are synonymous to giving the patient Robitussin® to control a cough. That is not a bad idea in and of itself. We can even argue which cough medicine may work best at controlling the cough. But the issue we face is not really a cough. What we are dealing with is PNEUMONIA! The Robitussin® may help control the cough in the short-term, but the patient is not going to get better.

Corporations spend $50 billion a year on leadership training and development and that number continues to grow. There are more leadership books than ever available for any aspiring or current leader to read. But leaders are not getting better. In a survey of over fourteen thousand leaders and HR professionals conducted every two years since 2009, Development Dimensions International (DDI) found that the effectiveness of leaders in business had not improved from 2009 to 2015. In fact, despite the increase in spending on leadership development, only one in three people believe they received value from the leadership training they got at work. Plus, only 15 percent of leaders in the survey rated their company's leadership bench strength as "high" in 2015. Even that was a *decline* from 18 percent in 2011.[1]

The results are in: *What we are doing to develop leaders is not working! We are treating the symptoms and ignoring the disease.*

One definition of insanity is doing the same thing over and over again and expecting different results. Let's stop treating a pneumonia patient with over-the-counter cough medicine! Let's treat the underlying cause of the cough and the other symptoms that go with this disease.

In leadership, the symptoms may be trust, poor communication, goal setting, employee turnover, coaching skills, or dysfunctional teams. But the underlying disease, the main issue that does not get adequately addressed, is CHARACTER. We are practicing leadership and developing leaders without an adequate consideration for character. To change our own results and to change the results of leadership development books and seminars, character must be at the foundation of every effort, or else we will keep missing the underlying cause of 90 percent of all our leadership woes.

---

1   *Global Leadership Forecast 2014/2015*, report from Development Dimensions International.

We believe that the *Habits of Character* that determine your strength of character as well as ours flow from two critical habits: *Courage* and *Humility*. Without *Courage* and *Humility*, the other critical habits we unpack in this book—*Integrity, Selflessness, Duty,* and *Positivity*—will continue to be well-meaning platitudes instead of character-changing behaviors.

Simple Truths Simply Presented

If you are like most leaders, you are overwhelmed with the demands of work and home life. We are not delusional and believe you have hours upon hours to wade through an academic treatise on leadership. So we did not write one. This book is designed so you can read a chapter and put it down. There is a free online character assessment available at (http://alslead.com/character-test) so you can evaluate which chapters you want to dig into and which ones you can read once and move forward. Or, you can read our book straight through and then return to the chapters you want to dwell on. We also have reflective questions for you to contemplate at the beginning of each chapter to help you focus on the topic at hand; you could spend a short time or a long time ruminating over those. Whatever works best for you.

Each chapter contains stories from the battlefields of Southeast Asia and the boardrooms of corporate America. These stories will open each chapter on the *Habits of Character* and create a foundation for our discussions.

Inside each chapter, you are going to get no-nonsense definitions of *Leader of Character*, character, and each of the six *Habits of Character*. When something can be said simply and briefly, that's just what we do. Then, with our terms defined, we dig into the six *Habits of Character* that all of us need and can grow into as *Leaders of Character*. These habits are not new, but they are certainly dynamic, and they will revolutionize your leadership and even the rest of your life.

At the end of each of the six character-habit chapters, we provide exercises— straightforward day-to-day and week-to-week activities that will act as character workouts. The best thing about these workouts is that you do not have to change your clothes and go to a gym to do them. You can do them wherever you are and with whomever you encounter.

All in all, what we provide in these pages are real-life practical solutions for growing as *Leaders of Character*. This book is designed for you to grow your own leadership influence. And it can also be used with your work teams and within your families. We do not just tell you what the six *Habits of Character* are. We also tell you how to develop those habits in yourself, in your team, and even in your family.

Who Are We?

The chronologically superior of us, General Jim Anderson (aka *The General*), spent forty-two years leading soldiers in the United States Army. He grew up in a county-run orphanage after being abandoned there by his father. The only way he could afford college was to go to the Naval Academy or to West Point. Realizing he got seasick too easily, he chose the Army.

After graduating from West Point, *The General* served as an infantry officer, an Army Ranger School instructor, and a veteran of two combat tours in Vietnam. He spent his final twenty-four years on active duty at West Point as the *Master of The Sword* (aka Head of the Department of Physical Education). *The General* devoted those years to developing our nation's future Army officer corps. He brings a military man's perspective to our conversation on leadership.

The younger of us, Dave Anderson (aka *The Business Guy*), also graduated from West Point. After serving in combat in Operation Desert Storm, he spent twenty years in a Fortune 50 company in sales and in various sales leadership positions. He is a corporate world business veteran who is now a professional speaker, talk-radio-show host, and consultant. His passion is for building *Leaders of Character* and building character in organizations large and small.

Our goal is to help you realize that your character is why people follow you. Who you are at your core impacts your effectiveness as a leader more than any management skill-based seminar or MBA program available. Besides, that MBA is a Masters of Business Administration, not a Master's of Business Leadership. And from what we see going on in business today, character-based leadership, not administration, is what our culture needs.

Are You Ready?

Imagine this. You are the leader everyone wants to work for and everyone wants to do business with. Why? Because people *want* to follow you. They know you are willing to make the hard decisions and are also humble enough to listen to feedback from others. They know your word is gold, and you always follow through on your promises. They know you want what is best for them and that you will always push them to grow beyond who they are today. In other words, they want a *Leader of Character* and that leader is you! Is that what you want for yourself? Are you ready to do what it takes to achieve that?

In families, companies, and countries throughout history, generation after generation has handed the baton of leadership to the next generation, hoping they were not only eager to run the race laid out for them but that they were ready to meet the challenge of leading. If you are part of that new generation, are you ready to run that race? And if you are among those soon to pass along the baton, are you ready to prepare those coming up behind you?

Maybe you are one of the young guns. You are whom our future depends upon. The future of your family, your company, and even your country is riding on what type of leader you will become. Are you ready to lead? We want to help you become the *Leader of Character* we all need you to be today and for decades to come.

Maybe you are in the leadership mix now. You are mid-career. You have survived up and down economies. You have worked for good and bad bosses. You are leading a small team or maybe a large organization. And in your leadership role, you know you have room to grow. You've read books and gone to seminars, but getting past the current demands of your life prevents you from truly implementing the stuff you read and heard from all those other authors and consultants. This book is designed to help you begin to grow as a *Leader of Character* today because you are needed today at your work, in your home, and for your country. Are you ready?

Perhaps you are the grizzled veteran of so many leadership battles you can't remember them all. You've had good years and bad years. You know the time is close at hand for you to hand the baton of leadership to someone else. Who should that person be? What should he or she be preparing for? How should you prepare this person? This book will help you pass that baton to a *Leader of Character* when the time is right, and it will help you learn how to model those behaviors from now until then. Are you ready?

Being a *Leader of Character* is not complicated, but it is hard. That is why we use exercise terminology throughout the book.

Our goal in this book is to provide the young guns a healthy exercise program that will defeat the disease before it can cause any damage. For those at the mid-career point, you will see a treatment plan and rehabilitation exercises that will repair any damage and help prevent the disease from recurring. For the grizzled veteran, what we lay out may be like a maintenance program. You've survived the ravages of the disease, and you do not want to risk going back there again. These are the exercises you must do so you do not succumb to the disease as you continue to mature.

Leadership Is Not Easy

> *"Being a professional is doing the things you love to do, on the days you don't feel like doing them."*
> – **Julius Erving** (Dr. J)

If you want to grow as a leader, you are going to have to put in the same effort as a great athlete or a great chef. The way forward is not going to be easy. Becoming a great leader, a great athlete, or a great chef takes more than desire or even knowledge. It takes effort. It takes practice. It takes hard work. It takes doing what you need to do on days you don't feel like doing it.

To grow you have to break a sweat. Growth—going beyond where you currently are—requires you to get uncomfortable and sweat. When most people head to the gym, they realize that to get any better, any stronger, or anymore fit, they will have to push past what is comfortable. Sweat and discomfort help us get fit. The same is true when it comes to leadership. To grow as a leader, you have to be willing to sweat and do uncomfortable things.

In other words, simply reading this book will not make you a *Leader of Character*. To become a great leader, you must become a great worker too. No one ever gets in shape by reading a fitness magazine or by going to the gym once. We get in shape by actually working hard consistently. We want you to do more than read the principles in this book. We want you to DO them.

You have to DO what you want to BE!

One of the simplest truths in the world is that we will never become good at anything unless we actually do that thing. Good intentions and the desire to be good at something are never enough to get us to the point where we are actually good.

We are going to present a path to you that may be new and may seem hard. Realize, though, that new things typically seem difficult. But if we never try tackling something that's new, we will never become anything beyond who we already are. Everything of value is hard before it gets easy. We must get started and then practice doing it until we become proficient. And to become truly great at something, we must practice over an extended period of time until that skill becomes a habit. It must become part of who we are to the point where it is almost an unconscious behavior. The great free-throw shooters in basketball don't think about the mechanics of shooting a ball while they put it into the air. They just shoot because their mechanics have become habitual due to practice, practice, practice.

When it comes to becoming a person of character, much less a leader who exhibits character, you must master the small steps first. As Winston Churchill observed many years ago:

> *"Character may be manifested in the great moments,*
> *but it is made in the small ones."*

That is how we become good at anything. That is how great athletes or great chefs become great. They practice. They strive to master the small steps, not just the big ones. And that is how we will become the *Leaders of Character* missing in our culture today. James Foude said it well:

> *"You cannot dream yourself into character. You must hammer and forge one for yourself."*

So, our challenge to you is this: If you want to grow as a *Leader of Character* but don't want to be uncomfortable or put in the effort to do it, then this book is not for you. Put it down and walk away.

If you are still reading, then we assume you are ready to DO what you need to DO in order to BE who you want to BE. You are ready to really work your muscles and grow. You want to be a leader, or you are currently leading somewhere and you want to get better. You want people to follow you and actually be enthusiastic while doing it. You want to make an impact on the people at work, at home, and anywhere else you find yourself serving. You want to be a *Leader of Character*. If that's you, then we believe that what you need is a simpler and more effective leadership approach than what you can currently find. You—in fact, all of us—need an approach to leadership that is timeless, maybe a little old-fashioned, but still gets to the heart of being a leader. You need a solution to the root cause of our leadership crisis and not just something that only deals with the symptoms of the disease. You need something that will create a clear path for your growth as a *Leader of Character*. You need something you can read in short bursts or over long weekends. You need something you can share with others. But most of all, you need something you can implement and that will make a difference in how you lead. You need a plan that works. The book you now hold is that plan.

You cannot dream yourself into character.
You must hammer and forge one for yourself.

While we focus a lot of this book on leading in the workplace, we believe that helping someone become a *Leader of Character* at work will transcend the workplace. If we can help leaders get better at work, they will be better husbands, better wives, and better parents. They will be better in their kids' schools, better in their churches, and better anywhere else they are serving. That is why *The General* is still pounding on podiums speaking about leadership while most of his contemporaries are well into their retirement. That is why *The Business Guy* left his comfortable corporate life to create a business dedicated to the leadership principles he learned from his dad, West Point, wise authors, and the school of hard knocks. That is why we wrote this book! We wrote it for you, but we wrote it for all of us. Because we all need *Leaders of Character* wherever we may live, work, and serve.

The Workout Plan Ahead

This book is a workout plan that will build your character muscles. We provide the plan, but you must provide the effort. So here's what you can expect as you work through this plan.

Part 1: The Why and the What

Part 1 focuses on *why* becoming a *Leader of Character* is critical and *what* needs to be done to become such a leader. We lay out the model we will use to develop the *Habits of Character* you need to become a *Leader of Character*. This section of the book is foundational to every other chapter and topic we address. It sets the stage for you to understand our approach and take the first steps toward developing the habits that will make you a leader people will want to follow.

Parts 2 and 3: The How

This is where you can read about each of the six *Habits of Character* you need to develop in order to become a *Leader of Character*. We don't just tell you why you need to have *Courage, Humility, Integrity, Selflessness, Duty,* and *Positivity*. We lay out a plan that explains *how* you can develop each of these essential habits.

Each chapter starts with some questions for you to answer. These questions are designed to focus you on the particular habit addressed in that chapter. This

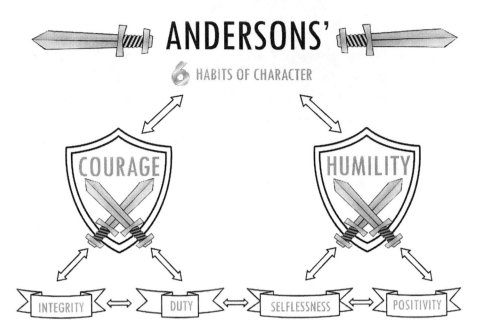

is the pre-workout stretching routine many of you are familiar with doing at the gym.

The remainder of each chapter is the workout itself. Some of the things we say may challenge your current perspectives or belief system. They may make you feel uncomfortable, which is okay. In fact, that is exactly what they are meant to do. We need to be uncomfortable to grow.

The final section of each chapter provides a list of exercises most of us can do daily and weekly to actually build up and strengthen the *Habit of Character* you just read about. Some of these exercises may be small activities, but they are meant to prepare you for the big character challenges you will certainly face at some point in leadership and in the other aspects of your life. They are exercises meant to prepare you and build those muscles so you are fit enough to respond well to a challenge.

Each chapter is designed to stand alone. If you are strong in one area but weaker in another, then read through the chapter that deals with your greater need and focus your development by using the exercises detailed at the end of that chapter. Stay in that chapter until you feel you have strengthened that *Habit of Character*.

Know as well that all six habits are interrelated. As the above "Andersons' Habits of Character" illustrates, the habits are all interconnected to some degree. If you work out one habit without regard for the others, you will be like the weight lifter who only does bicep curls or the runner who never lifts weights. Your lopsided routine may prepare you for one type of challenge, but it will not help you meet a host of other issues. We have set out for you a total leadership fitness plan. Accomplish it, and you will become healthy and strong in all areas of leadership.

We also believe that consistency is critical to developing each of these six habits.

- Unless we consistently act with courage, we likely are cowards.
- Unless we consistently act humbly, we probably think too much of ourselves.
- Unless we consistently act with integrity, we are not trustworthy.
- Unless we consistently do our duty, we are unreliable.
- Unless we consistently act selflessly, we probably are self-absorbed.
- Unless we consistently exhibit positivity, we probably drag others down.

Mastery requires a high level of consistency. And mastery brings its own rewards.

Part 4: DO What You Want to BE

In Part 4, you are going to see two vivid, living, personal examples of *Leaders of Character* in action. Where can we find individual *Leaders of Character* in today's world? How about the three women who became the first female soldiers to ever graduate from the US Army Ranger School. Where do you find a *Company of Character* in today's cut-throat business environment? We look at a franchise company with over 745 franchises in three countries and over $2.85 billion in annual revenue. Character works for them!

The final pages of Part 4 are our challenge to you. By the time you get to this point in the book, you will have bought in or not. If you have accepted what we say and are ready to apply it, the challenge we lay out for you will be the next steps you must take to begin to change our culture and to begin to DO What You Want to BE!

Appendices: Additional Support and Resources

In the very back of the book, there is one last place we designed for those of you who are ready to get going. We provide the appendices for those of you wanting more specifics on leading your families and your work teams to become *Families of Character* and *Teams of Character*.

You will also find a list of resources and websites we recommend for you so your learning does not end when you get to the last pages of this book.

As you master our plan for character-based leadership, our hope and prayer is that you will see the results that Jim Nipp, President of The Genesis Group, did. The Genesis Group is a multi-million-dollar telecommunications firm that develops tests and supports secure two-way voice and data systems. Dave worked with Jim and his firm on the approach to leadership that we have laid out in this book. Here is what Jim told us about the effectiveness of our leadership plan:

> Like most people in management, I spend a good deal of time in pursuit of the skills associated with leadership. I read books, I take seminars, I watch TED talks, I subscribe to various blogs from self-proclaimed leadership gurus, I read my Bible, I pray. What I had not done was create a plan of action and put in the work to become a leader that others actually wanted to follow. My experience with Dave, teaching many of the lessons learned from his father, made me realize that I had been much too passive in my pursuit of the "leader" title, without putting in the hard work required to actually change the course of my team and my company.
>
> Once we changed the coach (me), our team began to transform at every level. We changed our hiring practices, valuing character more than simply evaluating qualifications. We stopped avoiding difficult choices and began to hold everyone to the same high standards. We began to develop leaders at every level of our organization and have seen engagement and productivity skyrocket. We stopped talking about our

corporate culture and started finding ways to demonstrate it, both in business and in the community. Just like a January gym membership, this resolution would have been worthless if we hadn't committed, from the top down and from the bottom up, to make being "leaders of character" a part of our words and our actions—a habit.

Becoming a Leader of Character is like planting a tree. The best time to plant a tree was ten years ago. The next best time is right now.

If you are ready, your business, your family, and your country need *Leaders of Character* to step up and lead. So let's get started on growing into the *Leader of Character* all of us need. It is time to exercise and break a sweat!

Character may be manifested in the great moments,
but it is made in the small ones.

Character Assessment: http://alslead.com/character-test

PART 1

THE WHY AND THE WHAT

Chapter 2

LEADERS OF CHARACTER

The Warm-Up: Questions for Stretching Your Mind

Who is your Leadership Hero? _____

What three traits do you admire most about your Leadership Hero?
1. _____ *2.* _____ *3.* _____

The General: *Dave Palmer and the Purpose of West Point*

In 1986 Lieutenant General Dave Palmer arrived at West Point to serve as the Superintendent of the Military Academy. I was a professor and a member of the Academic Board. I remember that at one of the early Academic Board meetings in the fall of 1986, LTG Palmer asked us this question: "What is the purpose of the United States Military Academy?" The members of the board began spouting off their views. I did not say anything because I remembered that he had asked me that same question while I was visiting him that summer before it was announced that he would become the new Superintendent. After listening for a while, he asked us to go back to our offices and prepare a one-page paper in response to his question.

At future meetings we continued wrestling with our views and eventually came up with this statement of "The Purpose of USMA": "The purpose of the

United States Military Academy is to provide the nation with leaders of character to serve the common defense."

I recall that after that meeting when the new purpose statement was accepted, I returned to my office and began writing it on the top of a sheet of paper. When I got to the word "character" I had to stop. I began to question myself about the meaning of that word. I did not have a good definition.

My search led me to Plato and Aristotle. They had wrestled with the definition of character a long time ago. Plato, Aristotle's teacher, focused on ideas and ideals, while Aristotle believed that "Good character is the life of good conduct, right conduct in relation to other persons and in relation to one's self."

Prior to LTG Dave Palmer challenging the members of the Academic Board to develop the purpose of West Point, I had used the word character many times, but I had never given careful consideration to what the word really means. I have also found that most people who use the word have not given prior consideration to its meaning.

In my twenty-four years at West Point as a professor and member of the Academic Board, the development of that purpose statement was the most significant accomplishment of any of the twelve superintendents I served under. That purpose statement put the entire West Point training program into perspective. If something we were doing did not move our young men and women to become *Leaders of Character*, then there was no reason for us to be doing it.

The Business Guy: *What the People Follow*

For every audience I speak to, I have an audience participation portion. With each group, whether it is a group of 15 or 1,500, I ask them to think about their leadership hero. That person may be in history, in the movies, or someone for whom they have worked or played sports. Then I ask them these questions:

Who is your leadership hero? What is it you admire most about that leader?

We will touch on some of the answers from these groups in a moment, but first we want you to answer these questions for yourself. Who would you say is your leadership hero? And what are the top three traits you admire most about that person?

Your Leadership Hero: _____

Leadership Hero Top 3:

1._____2._____3._____

With a live audience, the answers to these questions always come fast and furious. I usually scribble the answers on a flip chart or white board. Here is an example from a recent group regarding the most admired traits:

Engaged	Trusts	Leads by example
Passionate	Builds trust	Empowers others
Optimistic	Work ethic	Unafraid
Open	Determined	Decisive
Respects others	Honest	

We posed those same two questions in a separate survey that included an online portion getting over six hundred responses. The top ten answers from the survey included:

Caring	Honesty	Listener
Compassionate	Humility	Passionate
Courage	Inspirational	Servant
Faith	Integrity	Wisdom

Now, look over these three lists: your Top 3, the list from my recent class, and the survey results. What do they show us? *People follow character.* In fact, the survey results found 87 percent of the answers listed character traits and not skills or competencies. No matter how many people I ask, no matter where in the business world I am, when people list what they admire most in great leaders, they describe character traits. Character more than competence is why people follow leaders. Who a leader is at his or her core is more important to followers than the skills that person brings to the table.

Defining *Leaders of Character*

"Character is higher than intellect."
    – **Ralph Waldo Emerson**

Leadership speaker and author John Maxwell jump-started the trend of defining leadership as influence. We agree with him and the leadership experts (such as Oswald Sanders) whom Maxwell cites as his inspiration. But does that definition go far enough? Does just having influence make someone a leader?

Along with influence, the direction we lead another person toward is important. Hitler had influence, but what he led people to do was horrific. Stalin had influence. Bin Ladin had influence too. But the goals of each of these leaders were immoral and incredibly damaging to generations upon generations of people. We believe that motives, among other things, separate the *Leaders of Character* from the rest.

We also maintain that there should be some level of achievement involved in leading. *Leaders of Character* are different than people who just wield influence. Who cares if I have influence on others, but the influence is not used to accomplish any concrete, beneficial goals?

A movie critic has influence, but whom are they leading? A talking head on CNN or Fox News has influence, but are they leading anyone towards something positive? Do they help others accomplish any goals?

No one would deny that Hitler and Jesus, Stalin and Ghandi, and Bin Ladin and Abraham Lincoln were leaders. They all had influence. But not all of them were *Leaders of Character*. Leadership—at least any leadership of genuine value—must be more than mere influence. It matters for what purpose that leadership is used, what goals are being pursued.

Andersons' 12-Word (or less) Definition of a Leader of Character
Someone who uses influence to achieve a moral or ethical goal

---

The type of goal a leader is aiming at defines whether he is a *Leader of Character* or just a person of influence. The bottom-line is this: when you try to differentiate a *Leader of Character* from the rest of the so-called leaders out there, look at their motives.

Andersons' Leadership Philosophy

COMPETENCE **LEADERSHIP** **CHARACTER**

Leadership is a blend of competence and character

The General: *Good Question*

My friend and West Point classmate General Norman Schwartzkopf helped me solidify my leadership philosophy. I was preparing to leave the military and was telling Norm about my plans to start my own leadership consulting business. That was when he asked me, "Jim, what's your niche?"

I told him my philosophy was that leadership was a blend of competence and character. He thought for a second and then added, "Jim, I agree. But did you ever stop to think that most failures in leadership are failures in character and not failures in competence?"

The bottom line is character is why people follow leaders. Another way to see this is to look at the biggest leadership failures we know. These could be people featured in the news, people from history, or people we personally know. When you think about those failures, were those failures in competence or as a result of character flaws?

Why Do Leaders Fail?

Fear, arrogance, lapses in integrity, selfishness, poor work ethic, bad attitudes—these are the causes of most leadership failures. Rarely is it a case that someone couldn't do the job due to competence issues. Usually it is a result of that leader having a character issue that caused their downfall.

- Did Nazi Germany collapse because Hitler and his party did not know how to run an efficient government or war machine? Or was it because Hitler was one of the most amoral and evil men of the twentieth century?
- Did Bernie Madoff's investment empire collapse because he didn't know how to manage money, or was it an issue of *Integrity*?
- Did Enron implode because the company leaders did not know how to run an energy trading company, or was it an *Integrity* issue? Or was it a *Courage* issue on the part of some leaders?
- Did FIFA not know how to promote soccer worldwide and how to generate an enormous fan base? Or was it the selfishness of the people indicted for fraud and corruption that put the whole organization in jeopardy?

Are we saying competence is not important? Absolutely not! Incompetence in a leader is incredibly damaging. Competency is a hugely important part of the leadership equation. Hiring, developing, and reinforcing leadership competence are critical for organizations and individuals to remain competitive. Leaders must be competent in certain management skills.

In fact, over and over again—in big and small businesses, in for-profits and non-profits, in the government and in the private sector—the search for and almost exclusive emphasis on competence reigns. We continue to hire, train, and evaluate people based on competencies. But, as we have repeatedly found, the inability to do the job is rarely why leaders fail—character is!

The Choice: Manager or *Leader of Character*

In many organizations, the terms *manager* and *leader* are used interchangeably. Maybe that is because management skills seem to be the focus of those organizations. Maybe these companies focus on management skills because they are easier to measure. But *Leaders of Character* know there is more to their jobs than just management.

Here are a few observations about *Leaders of Character* and managers.

- *Leaders of Character* **lead people, while management is about managing resources.** *Leaders of Character* know leadership is about people! The people make things happen. The people will have a larger impact on the bottom-line than will more money, better equipment, or shorter production cycles.
- *Leaders of Character* **grow leaders, while management is about maintaining processes.** Again, *Leaders of Character* know leadership is about people. If we are not developing people, we are not leading. The growth of the individuals on our team will ensure the long-term success of the team more than any well-managed and maintained process.

A *Leader of Character* never places resources, projects, or administrative tasks before people. Such leaders know that the work has to get done. But they know that people do the work and that people are more important than the work itself.

As important as people are, the majority of the leadership training that companies invest in focuses on the competencies of being a manager without regard for the character component that is critical to achieving individual and organizational excellence. These companies continue to give leaders the latest and greatest personality or strengths assessments, new coaching models, time management training, and many other topics related to managing and competency.

Leadership/Management Training Topics
from Three Prominent Companies

Setting Vision	Connecting with Team Members
Goal Setting	Coaching, Developing and Mentoring
Culture	Communication
Motivating Teams	Building Trust
Time Management	Generations in the Workplace
Recruiting and Hiring	Coaching for Performance
Conflict Resolution	Making Meetings Productive
Public Speaking	Finance for Non-Financial Managers
Increasing Team Productivity	Building Strong Teams

The training topics above can provide fantastic tools, but great tools do not necessarily make people great carpenters.

Good tools in the hands of the wrong people
often result in manipulation, not leadership.

If we want to be average, focusing on management development may be enough. But if we want to go beyond average and achieve excellence, then we must focus on becoming *Leaders of Character*. The same can be said for companies that focus on developing competencies without regard to the character component. Greatness will not be achieved through good management skills alone.

Which do you want to be: a proficient manager or a *Leader of Character*? The first creates compliant employees. The second leads committed followers!

In his groundbreaking book *Return on Character*, Fred Kiel studied CEOs who were rated high on employee-based character evaluations. The *Leaders of Character*, whom Kiel calls Virtuoso Leaders, led their companies to five times the return on assets than the leaders with lower character ratings.

Character is the determining factor in whether a team at work, an individual, or even a family will or will not follow you.

Which do you want to be: a proficient manager or a *Leader of Character?* The first creates compliant employees. The second leads committed followers!

The downfall of many leaders is not their ability to do the job, but who they are as a person. Who do their followers believe their leaders are at their core? Do the people see their leader as a *Leader of Character?*

To become a *Leader of Character* we must strengthen the critical *Habits of Character* so we are prepared for the challenges of leading. But what exactly is our character and how do we develop it? Read on and we will show you.

"Good character consists of knowing the good, desiring the good, and doing the good—habits of the mind, habits of the heart, and habits of action."
— **Thomas Lickona**

Character Assessment: http://alslead.com/character-test

Chapter 3

DEVELOPING OUR CHARACTER

The Warm-Up: Questions for Stretching Your Mind

1. *Who is the person with the highest character you know?*_____

2. *What does this person do (his or her behaviors) that demonstrates that character?* _____

3. *Who really knows what your character is?*_____

The General: *Who Really Knows Our Character?*

At the writing of this book, my wife Joyce and I have been married fifty-nine years. We began dating when I was sixteen years old and were married the day after I graduated from West Point in 1956. Except for the two-plus years I spent in Vietnam, we have never lived apart since we exchanged wedding vows at the Cadet Chapel at West Point.

I would say that we probably know each other as well as is possible for two people to truly know each other. But there are things she still does not know about me, and there are things I do not know about her. These are deep character things that only we know about ourselves.

I speak frequently as part of the faculty of the Lincoln Leadership Institute (LLI) in Gettysburg, PA. At LLI, I frequently ask the audience a question that you just answered for yourself: "Who really knows what your character is?" The answer: "Only I really know what my character is."

Defining *Character*

Character is a buzzword that we hear used over and over again. When it is used in politics or sports, *character* is rarely defined. Politicians talk about their character. Coaches talk about athletes being a "high character" recruit. But what is character?

If we asked a room full of people to define *character*, we would likely get a different answer from each person. We all use the word, but we rarely explain what we mean by it. To get a handle on this term, we need to go back to one of the greatest philosophers in history, Aristotle.

He and his teacher Plato spent a lot of time contemplating the topic of character. They used the word *ethos,* the Greek word from which we get the word *ethics. Ethos* is often translated as "character." Even though both *ethics* and *character* come from the same root word, they are not the same thing.

In the business world, ethics usually gets boiled down to a list of prescribed rules. Meeting these minimum expectations is considered ethical behavior. Many companies and industries have a code of ethics that tells everyone involved what not to do. This list of "don't do's" is meant to keep us in line and help us avoid being a bad person in the workplace.

Our ethics certainly play a part in our character, but ethics and character are not the same. We can claim to be ethical because we behave in accordance with the prescribed lists of "don't dos" and yet we can still have flaws in our character. Character goes beyond ethics. Our character describes something about us that our ethical views or our ethical rule-following may not touch. You see, our character displays *who we are at our core.*

Who we are at our core is where Plato and Aristotle disagreed. Plato believed that who we are is determined by what we think about or read about. In other words, Plato believed your character was about what knowledge you had about right and wrong. Aristotle, on the other hand, felt his teacher did not take the viewpoint far enough. Who we are goes deeper than what we think about or read about. Aristotle said that your *ethos*—your character—is about your habits.

In fact, perhaps the most literal translation of *ethos* from the Greek is the word *habit*. More specifically, in his *Nicomachean Ethics,* Aristotle reasoned that moral virtue is acquired only through practice. You become "just by doing just acts … you become brave by doing brave acts, you learn virtue by following rules of good behavior, hearing stories of virtuous people, and imitating virtuous models."

We think Aristotle was right. Our character is more about what we do on a regular basis than what we think about or talk about. Our habits, the good ones and the bad ones, determine our character. In other words, who I *think* I am is not who I am. Who I *say* I am is not who I am. Character is this: *who I am at my core is displayed through my habitual behaviors.*

Andersons' 12-Word (or less) Definition of Character
Our habitual way of operating: HOW we are is WHO we are!

Some common synonyms for character: personality, nature, disposition, temperament, mentality, makeup, honor, rectitude, uprightness

Character is more than simply following a list of prescribed rules. To become *Leaders of Character*, we must strive to achieve something that will always keep us on a higher path than just being an ethical rule follower. If we settle for that standard, we are setting our sights too low. What happens when we can't find a rule to govern our behavior in a particular situation? What will we do then? As *Leaders of Character,* we must develop the character that will guide us to make the right choices no matter the situation or the inadequacy of the rules.

Developing Character

Plato was not completely wrong in his understanding of character. Our thoughts do play a role in developing our character, but we need to go much deeper than that. As we see it:

- Our character starts with our ***thoughts***.
- Our thoughts influence our ***words***.

- Our words lead us to our *actions*.
- Our actions, repeated over time, become our *habits*.
- Our habits form our *character*.

Let's consider each of these steps toward developing our character.

Step 1: Our Thoughts

We all have good thoughts and bad thoughts. When another driver cuts us off on a busy street, some of the things that go through our heads may not be pretty. If we say what we are thinking, we impact our character. Our thoughts and what we do with them are the first step toward developing our character.

What we fill our heads with does affect who we are. If we watch pornography or read social media posts about Islamic jihad, those things influence us. Time spent in those things is why so many young people have an unhealthy attitude toward sex and why some of them are actually joining terrorist organizations in the name of jihad. Similarly, if we rarely read or if what we read is all fiction or pulp entertainment magazines, we are probably not growing as a person. But if we read biographies of great leaders, or books, blogs, or periodicals on leadership, or read the timeless leadership lessons in the Bible, we are preparing ourselves for growth. If we take opportunities to learn by attending seminars or listening to podcasts, we are setting the stage for our personal growth as well. We all should deliberately carve out time for more positive brain food.

We are not saying that every spare moment you have should be used for filling your mind with stuff that is good for you. Even *The General* and *The Business Guy* can watch *SportsCenter* over and over again. Still, the fact remains: what all of us fill our heads with does influence *who* we are and who we will become.

At the same time, just reading material that's good for you will not automatically make you a person of strong character. For example, we know plenty of people who claim to read the Bible. But even though they read the Bible's ageless wisdom, their behaviors don't reflect what they read. The same can be said for written codes of ethics. Just because your company has a code of ethics on the wall or a form people must sign that proves they read the code does not guarantee that good behavior will follow. Knowledge in and of itself is inadequate to generate character. But we cannot become people of character unless we have knowledge of what character is and how it can be developed.

Our point is this: whether we fill our minds with positive messages or negative ones, those messages will influence who we are and how we think. HOW we are is WHO we are. *The thoughts we have are the first step to who we are.*

Step 2: Our Words

The more we think about something, the more likely we are to speak that way. For example, the more times we look at material on the internet that degrades women, the more likely we are to speak about women in a degrading way.

Guys have all spent time in a locker room. The locker room is a haven for crass talk and sexual bravado. Much of that talk is degrading to the way men look at women. Involvement in those discussions creates a culture that inspires action, and those actions are often negative. For instance, the reputation of the NFL and its players are suffering for it. As more and more NFL players are accused of sexual misconduct or abuse of women, we cannot ignore the impact that "locker room talk" may be having on those players.

On the positive side, the ideas of a few learned men that became the themes of the American Revolution began just the same way. The ideas of the few spawned meetings in taverns and churches. These ideas of freedom and no taxation without representation were debated. The more people discussed these principles, the more inevitable action became.

Our words lead us to our actions. The American Revolution started with good ideas, but it was people gathering and speaking about these ideas that produced actions. Alcoholics Anonymous (AA), Weight Watchers, and churches use the same system to change people's habits and thus their lives. These organizations have proven the power of words in changing behaviors for the positive. They also prove that thoughts and knowledge by themselves are not enough to alter behaviors.

When a recovering alcoholic suffers a relapse, one of the first questions his sponsor asks is "Have you been going to your meetings?" Sponsors don't ask if you read the warning labels on a beer can or if you read the AA educational materials.

Similarly, at Weight Watchers, they don't just hand you a diet plan and say, "Now go lose weight!" They insist you come to weekly meetings as well, because they know the power words have in changing your behavior. The more we speak about something, the more likely our actions will follow that same path.

Churches buy into this as well. Most churches encourage their attendees to join a Bible study. They also know that many people who claim to read the Bible have not shown significant changes in their behaviors. But one reason this often occurs is because many of those who claim to read the Bible do not spend time discussing those lessons with other people. Churches know that group discussion is often the catalyst needed to change behaviors.

Just writing, reading, or watching inspiring works rarely spurs people to action. It is the gathering of two or more together to discuss those principles that creates momentum to overcome the inertia that our current comfort zones use to hold us back from initiating change.

A critical step to ensuring our character development is discussing what good looks like so that we are more likely to act that way in the future. That is how Plato trained his students such as Aristotle. Plato put his explanations of and arguments for virtue in the form of written dialogues. And these dialogues occurred with others listening in and sometimes joining in. As his student, Aristotle knew how virtue was learned because he not only heard it taught, but he also saw it discussed and practiced, and he participated in these lessons too.

Following rules, hearing stories, and imitating virtuous people all require discussions with others. Aristotle believed that you learn virtue by following rules of good behavior, hearing stories of virtuous people, and imitating virtuous models.

This approach to changing behavior is as effective today as it was centuries ago. For instance, the more an alcoholic talks with others about how she needs to avoid situations that trigger her drinking, the more likely she is to make the right choice when faced with temptation. The more an overweight man talks with others about avoiding restaurants or certain aisles in the grocery store, the more likely he is to choose the salad bar or the fresh vegetables section when shopping. The more consistently we discuss the ideas shared at church or in Bible studies, the more likely we are to act in alignment with those principles when we are faced with choices in the future.

But thinking and talking about what we should do or what ought to be done is not character. Having character takes action. Character is the sum total of our habits, the good ones and the bad. But before we develop habits, we have to make those initial choices. We have to take action.

Step 3: Our Actions

The life-long pursuit of knowledge is worthless unless we do something with that knowledge. Likewise, sitting around with others and talking about what should be done can be just as empty. Without action, the study and the discussion are just a waste of our time. Or even worse. The accumulation of knowledge for the sake of accumulating knowledge can be an act of pride and selfishness. Some individuals use it to pump up their own egos and self worth. Let's be honest. Who cares how much we know, or how many books we have read, or how many sermons we have heard, or how many degrees we have earned, if we never put feet on what we have learned? If we never put what we know into action, then what use is that knowledge?

Knowledge without action is worthless.
But knowledge with action puts us on the path to wisdom.

Our thoughts lead us to our words, and our words lead us to our actions. The more we talk about something, the more likely we are to act in that way. And each time we take action—each time we make a choice to act—we make it easier to make that same choice again the next time. But it all begins with that critical first choice:

- The choice to avoid that drink or ignore that leftover pizza
- The choice to join others in protest or to fight for the rights you feel are being denied

- The choice to tell the truth to your wife or husband, even though it may make them angry

Each of these choices sets us on a path to a new habit or reinforces an old one. Each time we make a choice, we make it easier to make the same choice again in the future. But choosing to do something once does not change who we are in the long run. Consistently choosing something is what creates a habit. Just because you smoke a cigarette once does not make you a smoker. But if you choose to smoke another cigarette and another and another, soon you will have formed a habit. Each time you choose the cigarette, it makes it easier to choose it the next time and the next and the next. Likewise, just because you tell the truth once in a while does not make you a person of *Integrity*. But, if you choose to tell the truth once, and then do it again and again on a consistent basis, *Integrity* will become your habit. Each time you act with *Integrity*, it will make it easier to choose to act with *Integrity* the next time you are tested and the next.

That is how habits are formed—one decision at a time.

Step 4: Our Habits

Your actions repeated over time form your habits. All habits begin with one decision. That first decision can set you on a path toward a positive habit or a negative one. Your habits are formed one decision at a time.

How many people have started a workout program? Most of us have. The toughest morning is the first morning. If we drag ourselves out of bed that first morning and go for that jog or attend that Zumba® class, it makes it easier the next morning to make that choice again. After a few weeks, we have a habit formed. Without thinking, when our alarm wakes us, we turnoff our alarm, put on our workout clothes, and head out the door.

But what about when that morning comes and it is raining outside? Or it's the morning after you were awake until 2 a.m. with your restless child? Our temptation is to hit that snooze button, turn over, and go back to sleep. Now, hitting the snooze button at that moment is not wrong. It truly is a morally neutral choice. But what does that set you up for the following morning? For getting out of bed, or staying in bed once again?

That's why we asked if you ever *started* a workout program before. Because most of us have faced that morning when it is hard to get up. That morning when if feels so good to sleep in. And that first morning is usually the beginning of the end of our fitness regime. It is the end to that new habit we had formed or were trying to form.

In the same way, just because you tell the truth once does not make you an honest person. Just because you tell the truth when it is convenient does not make you an honest person. You are an honest person if honesty is your habit. If you consistently make the choice to tell the truth when you are faced with the temptation to do the opposite, then you can consider yourself an honest person because it is what you consistently do. It has become your habit.

Step 5: Our Character

All of this is great news! If our character is formed by our habits, we should feel relieved! That means we can start to change our character today. The process of changing our character begins by making a new choice today. If, for example, you are currently struggling over how easy it is for you to tell a lie or to act selfishly, then you can begin to transform your character by making a new decision the next time you are tempted. Changing or strengthening your character does not take a crazy act of bravery or an epiphany of enormous proportions. What it takes is a new decision. Once you make a new choice, then you are on the road to changing your character. Character Assessment: http://alslead.com/character-test

Character Assessment: http://alslead.com/character-test

I can become unselfish even if I have been a selfish prig my entire life. I can become a man of *Integrity* even if I have lied every day since my childhood. I can become a glass-half-full guy even if I have been the chronic complainer. I can become the person who owns my screw-ups even if I am traditionally a world-class excuse-maker. I can become a warm and caring individual even if I have been a cold-hearted piece of granite in the past. Each of these transformations can start today—for you and for me. It starts with one choice in the right direction, and it becomes a habit one choice at a time.

Are you willing to make that choice? Are you willing to upgrade the person you have been to become the person you always wanted to be? Are you ready to become the leader people want to follow? Are you ready to lead in a way that allows you to sleep contentedly at night? That is the *Leader of Character* this book aims at identifying. That is the *Leader of Character* we describe in Part 2. That is the *Leader of Character* each of us can become for our families, our businesses, our communities, our ministries, and our country.

How can this be done? Is there a model for developing character that we can replicate for ourselves, for our teams, for our families?

West Point's Honor Education: The Character Development Model

The purpose of West Point Military Academy is described this way:

> "The purpose of the United States Military Academy is to provide the nation with *Leaders of Character* to serve the common defense."

The entire educational experience at West Point is designed to prepare young men and women to be *Leaders of Character* who will lead our soldiers and our country. But, West Point was founded as an engineering school. In fact, as recently as September 22, 2015, *US News and World Report* rated West Point as the third ranked engineering school in the country. Robert Sterling in the magazine *American Enterprise* reported that the academies (Army, Navy, Air Force) had produced over 1,531 corporate CEOs, 2,012 corporate presidents, and well over 5,000 vice presidents, not to mention thousands of small company entrepreneurs from the end of World War II through 2000.[2] In 2014 *USA Today* reported that West Point had the highest paid business graduates among all US universities.[3] We found this especially interesting, since West Point does not

---

2   Robert Sterling, "Meet America's Best Business Schools," *American Enterprise*, 11:5 (July/August 2000), 44.

3   Carly Stockwell, "The 10 Colleges with the Highest Paid Business Graduates," *USA Today*, August 15, 2014, http://college.usatoday.com/2014/08/15/the-10-colleges-with-the-highest-paid-business-graduates/.

offer any business-related majors. In the *American Enterprise* article, Sterling concluded that the education that the future business leaders received at West Point was more important to their success outside of the military than were the MBAs that many of them earned later in life.

I, *The Business Guy*, concur with what *American Enterprise* concluded. My MBA was useful in helping me understand the language of business and other areas like marketing, finance, and accounting. I also learned some managerial and administrative skills that helped me run a business. But my MBA courses provided little to no discussion about leading people. Ninety percent of the classes focused on management competencies.

Some people may call West Point an engineering school or a business school, but at its heart West Point is a leadership school, just as the Purpose of West Point claims.

While everything at West Point is meant to prepare cadets to be *Leaders of Character*, the school's Honor Code is the cornerstone of that development. The Honor Code states, "A cadet will not lie, cheat, or steal, nor tolerate those who do." The Honor Code is not a set of rules and regulations meant to create compliant cadets. It is not designed to make sure cadets follow the rules. Rather, the Honor Code is meant to change who cadets are at their core. The Honor Code was created and implemented to turn young cadets into honorable *Leaders of Character*.

> The Honor Code states, "A cadet will not lie,
> cheat, or steal, nor tolerate those who do."

Of course, honor codes are not unique to West Point or the other military service academies. You can find honor codes at the Ivy League schools and at a number of state schools. Many prep schools and public high schools are adopting honor codes too. To all of this we say "Bravo"! But have behaviors among students changed?

US News and World Report cites studies showing 64 percent of high school students admit to cheating on tests and 82 percent cheated on homework assignments.[4] In another often cited study, at least 75 percent of college students admit to cheating at some point in their academic career.[5] The statistics among graduate students are not much better.

Advanced Degrees in Cheating

Graduate school students who admit to cheating[6]:

- 56 percent of MBA students
- 54 percent of Master's in Engineering
- 48 percent of Master's in Education
- 45 percent of law school students

If we take each group individually, we can draw some disturbing conclusions:

- ✓ More than half of the future business leaders with MBAs may falsify financial performance in order to make their performance look better than it is.
- ✓ More than half of the engineers with master's degrees may be willing to fake critical safety data when designing a building, an aircraft, or a bridge.
- ✓ Almost half of all master's-qualified educators may cheat in order to make their classroom, school, or school district performance look better.
- ✓ Almost half of all the lawyers that are supposed to represent and fight for justice, many of whom becoming governmental leaders, may lie and cheat to reach their personal and career goals.

---

4   Eddie Ramirez, "Cheating on the Rise among High School Students," *US News and World Report*, December 2, 2008.
5   James M. Lang, "How College Classes Encourage Cheating," *Boston Globe*, August 4, 2013.
6   Alan Finder, "34 Duke Business Students Face Discipline for Cheating," *New York Times*, May 1, 2007, A15.

Since so many students are behaving dishonorably, what's missing in our institutions of learning? And why haven't the honor codes at other institutions had the same impact on the character of students as West Point's Honor Code has? The answer is profound: West Point's goal is not compliance; instead, West Point's purpose is to develop character, which includes compliance to its Honor Code. You see, the Honor Code is not the highest level of character-based behavior cadets are expected to achieve. It is the minimum standard. When the Honor Code does not specifically address an ethical dilemma, cadets and officers need to be able to make the wise and moral decision to do the right thing even though there may not be a rule prohibiting a particular behavior. Being a person of high character does not begin and end with following the rules. Cadets know you can be an unethical rule-follower. The honor education system helps cadets take the Code's minimum standard to another level in the pursuit of truly developing into *Leaders of Character*.

Mike Krzyzewski, more famously known as Coach K, is a 1969 graduate of West Point. While there, he got the message about rules and character. He teaches, "Rules are no substitute for character." When you play basketball for him, it's your character that matters most.

"Rules are no substitute for character."

How does West Point develop character beyond just enforcing the rules? By focusing on developing *Habits of Character*. In order to achieve that goal, West Point uses Aristotle's model for character development. The Academy wants cadets who go beyond compliantly following the rules to become leaders who are committed to making honorable choices on a habitual basis.

Cadets are not handed a copy of the Honor Code and told, "Now go out there and be honorable." Unfortunately, that is what many companies, colleges, and families do with their regulations, codes, and rules. In fact, a 2010 survey at Yale University found that more than half of its undergraduate students never even read the school's policies on academic honesty.[7] One wonders if it would have made much difference if they had.

At West Point, there is an honor education system in place that goes well past impacting a cadet's thoughts by just giving him or her the Honor Code. The next critical step is in the form of Honor classes. Cadets meet consistently in small groups throughout their four years at West Point for classes that are case-study based. Most of the case studies center around real-life scenarios cadets and officers have and will face as leaders. As freshmen and sophomores, the focus is on living honorably in cadet life. They discuss temptations, such as cheating on tests, using work from others without citing sources, and cadet borrowing (borrowing an item from a classmate without intending to return it). In each case there is a critical decision they are asked to debate and defend. These are not easy discussions. Many times these cases involve turning in a friend who may have violated the Honor Code. The toleration clause claims that if a cadet knows someone else violated the Honor Code and does nothing, the person who stays silent is also guilty of an honor violation and may also face expulsion from the Academy.

As juniors and seniors, the emphasis moves to living honorably as part of the larger Army officer corps. The discussions center on scenarios and challenges officers will face with subordinates, peers, and superiors in peacetime and in battle.

These are tough choices discussed in a safe environment. These discussions ask cadets to face their preconceived notions about their own character and what standards they have for acting with *Integrity*. They force cadets to think well beyond the immediate impact of a decision to the ripple effects that compromising their *Integrity* can have in the long run. In other words, cadets are flexing the muscles in these practice sessions that they will need for making a wise decision when the real tests of their character come later in life.

Just like Aristotle's model, these discussions are designed with the idea that the more we speak about making wise choices, the more likely we are to act in that way. As honor, character, and *Integrity* become consistent and frequent topics,

---

7   Richard Perez-Pena, "Studies Find More Students Cheating, with High Achievers No Exception," *New York Times*, September 7, 2012.

cadets are increasingly more prepared to make the tough character decisions that they are sure to face in the future. At West Point, each time cadets make a wise and tough decision and choose "the harder right instead of the easier wrong," as the Cadet Prayer states, it becomes easier to make the same choice again. As they choose the harder right more and more often, doing the right thing becomes a *Habit of Character* that becomes part of who they are.

We are not naïve. Most cadets begin with the mindset of complying with the Honor Code because they do not want to be thrown out of school. But as the honor education system works, the decisions cadets may have made in their heads as freshmen or sophomores become decisions they make in their hearts as upperclassmen and as part of the Army officer corps.

Unlike a lot of the other prestigious schools that have honor codes, West Point takes its code beyond the mere development, publishing, and enforcement stages. Honor discussions do not happen only at freshmen orientation week or once a year. The cadet honor education system is a consistent presence in the life of cadets. As a result, *the Honor Code is not something that is complied with but something committed to* by the overwhelming majority of graduating cadets.

At West Point, other educational institutions, in businesses, and in families, we cannot set up enough rules to prevent every unethical behavior. The honor codes at schools, codes of ethics in businesses, and the "family rules" can only cover so much. Developing character using West Point's model creates wise decision-makers versus compliant rule followers.

The honor education system established at West Point helps young men and women from all over the United States, with different worldviews and varied family structures, become *Leaders of Character* who develop the *Habits of Character* we unpack throughout the rest of this book. The system has worked for more than two hundred years, and it is the format we propose for leaders, organizations, and families who want to develop their character and the character of those they have the most contact with.

Courage, Humility, Integrity, Selflessness, Duty, and *Positivity* are all *Habits of Character* we can develop no matter our worldview, cultural influences, or family backgrounds. These are the *Habits of Character* that work together to make us the leaders people want to follow and the leaders that will change the current direction of leadership in our culture today. By moving in this direction, we will become the new counterculture. We will become the *Leaders of Character* our culture so desperately needs.

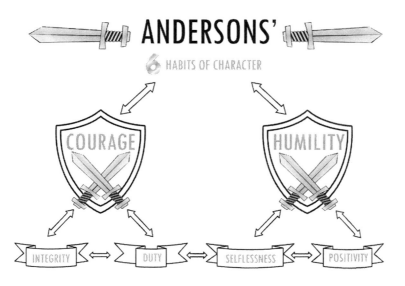

Cherokee Parable: Two Wolves

One evening an old man told his grandson about a battle that goes on inside people. He said, "My son, the battle is between two 'wolves' inside us all.

"One is Evil. It is anger, envy, jealousy, sorrow, regret, greed, arrogance, self-pity, self-absorption, guilt, resentment, inferiority, lies, pride, superiority, and ego.

"The other is Good. It is joy, peace, love, hope, serenity, humility, kindness, benevolence, empathy, generosity, truth, compassion, and faith."

The grandson thought about it for a minute and then asked his grandfather, "Which wolf wins?"

The old man simply replied, "The one you feed."

Character Assessment: http://alslead.com/character-test

PART 2

THE FOUNDATIONAL HABITS

Introduction

WHY COURAGE AND HUMILITY COME FIRST

If character is the reason most leaders fail, what causes most of our character failures? Why do some leaders succumb to the temptation to lie or cheat? Why do others avoid confrontations or demean their subordinates? Why do micromanagers micromanage? Honestly, most resources do not go deep enough and get to the root cause of these failures. They just say, "Don't do this," or "Do this instead." We realized we needed a different approach. We wanted to find the real cause for character failures, and we think we found the cause—actually, two causes!

As we began to outline this book and determine the six *Habits of Character* leaders need to develop to become *Leaders of Character*, we placed *Integrity* at the very top of the list. We were not alone. Over and over again, great leadership experts and best-selling leadership books place *Integrity* first. This makes sense. *Integrity* is a critical *Habit of Character* that will determine whether people trust you, believe in you, and follow you.

Still, through our study on the topic of *Integrity* and through our own lives and observing the lives of other leaders, we recognized that to have *Integrity* we must first have *Courage*. Fear is constantly working inside of us, convincing us to stay quiet because some action or choice is not worth the risk. That led us to ask, "Is it truly *Integrity* if we only tell the truth when there is no risk involved?"

Fear prevents a lot of people from stepping forward and doing the right thing. Therefore, *Integrity* requires *Courage*! The great eighteenth-century British statesman Edmund Burke once said, "The only thing necessary for the triumph of evil is for good men to do nothing." And many times good men and women do nothing because they lack the needed *Courage* to step out and challenge evil.

"The only thing necessary for the triumph of evil
is for good men to do nothing."

With that revelation, we looked at other topics on leadership and realized that *Leaders of Character* must have *Courage* to engage in positive conflict, to trust their people, or to put the needs of others ahead of their own needs.

Then we asked ourselves, "What other character flaws are at the root of most failures?" When we looked at issues such as micromanaging, arrogance, not listening to others, selfishness, and bad attitudes, the common denominator in those failures involved pride. In the Judeo-Christian tradition, pride was the original sin that caused Adam and Eve to eat the fruit God had forbidden them to eat in the Garden of Eden. You don't have to be a Jew or a Christian to know that pride is present in all of us to some degree. Pride emerges in the form of either arrogance or insecurity, which are really two sides of the same coin. And they are the root cause of many leadership failures. Pride is an insidious character flaw that contributes to our leadership failures and our personal failures as well.

The opposite of pride is *Humility*. This virtuous habit is critical to becoming a *Leader of Character* and exhibiting *Habits of Character*, such as *Duty, Selflessness,* and *Positivity*.

Consider the items below:

Integrity	Listening skills
Trust	Open communication
Conflict resolution	Selflessness
Coaching and developing others	Empowering others

Accountability	Mentoring others
Holding others accountable	Performance management
Results orientation	Delegating
Attitude	

These traits and behaviors can be found on lists of core competencies many companies embrace. Human resource departments develop these for management classes that training departments teach. These are all leadership topics that companies, consultants, and authors try to address in order to improve leaders.

We can make an argument that fear and pride are the root cause for most of the failures experienced in the above areas. It doesn't matter how these failures present themselves, whether in areas of integrity, trust, conflict resolution, or others. If we want to change the effectiveness of our leadership development efforts, we have to start at the root cause of the issues: fear and pride.

To effectively counteract fear and pride, we must begin with the critical development of *Courage* and *Humility*—the two character habits that directly defeat fear and pride. If we fail to do this, we will keep treating the symptoms of leadership failures rather than their causes. You see, we believe that 90 percent of all our failures in character can be traced back to an issue of fear or pride. This is why Part 2 of this book focuses on the habits of *Courage* and *Humility*. We contend that without these two *Habits of Character*, the other habits we explore in Part 3—*Integrity, Selflessness, Duty, and Positivity*—are not possible. To some degree or another, *Courage* and *Humility* play a role in determining which *Habits of Character* we excel in or fail in. We can all look back at our lives and see failures large and small. When we work our way down to the root cause of most of those failures, fear or pride and sometimes both are usually present. That is why *Courage* and *Humility* come first in this book.

We begin with *Courage*.

Character Assessment: http://alslead.com/character-test

Chapter 4

HABIT #1: COURAGE

The Warm-Up: Questions for Stretching Your Mind

Who is the bravest person you know? _____

When you see a soldier in a movie turn and run instead of staying and fighting, what is your immediate reaction? _____

On a scale of 1 to 10, with 10 being the bravest, how brave are you? _____

> *"Courage is not simply one of the virtues, but the form of every virtue at the testing point."*
> — **C. S. Lewis**, *The Screwtape Letters*

The General: *The Bravest Thing I Ever Saw*

The Ambush
In October 1963, I was a captain deployed in the Delta of Vietnam. I was there as an advisor to a Vietnamese Battalion of the 15th Infantry Division. Prior to serving in Vietnam, I was an Instructor at the US Army Ranger School. Because

of my specialized training in guerilla warfare tactics, I was sent to Vietnam to help teach the South Vietnamese Army how to stay out of ambushes led by the North Vietnamese Army (NVA) and the Viet Cong soldiers.

On October 20, Dai Wei Mihn, the battalion commander of the battalion I was advising, was informed that the chief of Long Huu village had asked for a resupply of ammunition. Our battalion was given the mission of delivering the ammunition to Long Huu, which is located in Sadec Province in the Delta of Vietnam.

After a discussion of the mission, we decided to send out two companies of infantry during the night to establish security positions on both our flanks. The next morning, we cleared the mines along the dirt berm that was to be our route through the rice paddy to Long Huu, while our fourth company moved the ammunition forward to our battalion command post.

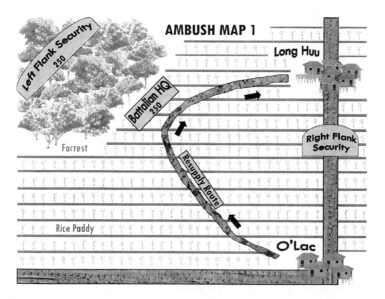

At about the time when we were ready to move the ammunition the last mile to Long Huu, the security company on our left flank opened fire on a large force of NVA and Viet Cong enemy soldiers moving toward our battalion headquarters. Simultaneously, enemy soldiers in the vicinity of Long Huu opened fire on our company that was moving through the rice paddies toward Long Huu in order to deliver the ammunition.

After a discussion with Dai Wei Mihn, we decided to have the right flank security company attack the enemy near Long Huu that was firing on our company, which was in the exposed position in the rice paddy.

However, we still had a problem on our left flank. The left flank security company was slowly withdrawing back to the vicinity of the battalion headquarters, giving us about five hundred soldiers to defend the headquarters and protect the rear of the company in the rice paddy. We knew we were in trouble and about to be overrun and be killed or captured. After the battle, we found out that the attacking enemy force was about one thousand five hundred strong. We were outnumbered three to one.

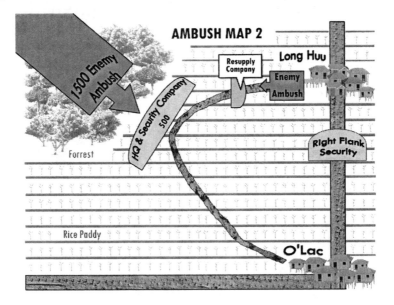

In the heat of the action, Dai Wei Mihn and I decided that we needed to do something to surprise the enemy. Remembering the success Joshua Chamberlain had on Little Round Top at the Battle of Gettysburg a hundred years earlier when his unit was about to be destroyed, we decided to fix bayonets and charge directly into the larger enemy force. As Dai Wei Mihn pulled his .45 caliber pistol out of his holster, he called out to his soldiers to fix bayonets. I saw that his soldiers were complying, and I fixed my bayonet onto my CAR 15 rifle.

That is when Dai Wei Mihn did one of the bravest, most courageous things I ever saw on a battlefield. He climbed over the berm we were behind and started walking alone toward the advancing enemy. My job was to stay with him, so I climbed over the berm with him. He paused for a moment as bullets whistled by us and yelled for his soldiers to follow him. He then resumed walking toward the attacking enemy force with his .45 outstretched. That is when those five hundred soldiers came over the berm yelling and screaming and running right at the enemy. Caught by surprise and no doubt amazed that a clearly outnumbered unit would charge directly into the teeth of a superior force, the NVA and Viet Cong soldiers turned and ran away.

This battle was the first recorded time a South Vietnamese force had ever defeated an enemy ambush. The whole battle lasted about eighteen hours before we were able to consolidate our position and care for our dead and wounded.

Those actions by Dai Wei Minh set the example for his soldiers. The *Courage* he displayed was a vivid, living, personal example to all of us. His soldiers followed him that day, not because he told them what to do, but because he showed them what to do, showing them what *Courage* looked like in action.

The Business Guy: *Scared to Speak Up*

I consulted with a large company at one point where mid-level leaders were hesitant to speak up when they saw a problem because they believed they would get fired if they did. So many people believed this would happen that it paralyzed the entire leadership team and each of their departments.

One day, in a room of thirty mid-level leaders, we determined they averaged fifteen years of experience with the company. Once that was determined, I asked how many people knew for a fact that someone had ever been fired by upper management for speaking up. Crickets could be heard chirping. Not a single person in that room actually knew of someone getting fired for such an act. We are talking 450 years of combined experience in that room. Yet they all believed they would lose their jobs if they exposed a problem. Their perception of risk made them fearful, and fear kept them from acting.

Without *Courage* we will never develop the other *Habits of Character*, such as *Integrity*, *Selflessness*, *Duty*, and *Positivity*. *Courage* is needed to overcome our daily fears so we can build up the muscles of character we will all need when faced with the character challenges that are in our future.

Defining *Courage*

The word *courage* is a commonly used term to describe a lot of different behaviors. But *courage* is rarely defined by the people using it. *Courage* is another word that deserves a definition so that we know what we are working toward.

Andersons' 12-Word (or less) Definition of Courage
Acting despite perceived or actual risk

Some common synonyms for *courage*: bravery,
valor, mettle, fortitude, tenacity, backbone, guts

Why do we specifically identify both perceived and actual risk? One word: experience. *The Business Guy's* story above serves as just one example of perceived risk. Take a minute to look back over the last thirty days of your life and recall the things that caused you anxiety. We are talking about the "what if" scenarios that floated through your brain and caused you to wring your hands in worry. Now ask yourself, "How many of those what-ifs actually came to fruition?" Most people would say very few. You see, we worry about a host of scenarios, most of which never occur. But many people sit on their hands and do nothing because of a perceived risk that is highly unlikely to ever happen. Those people let the perception stop them from acting and thus stop them from stepping forward and leading. They let the uncertainty and anxiety that emerge in the boardrooms block them from moving forward. Which is ironic considering that the reason leaders are relied upon and paid more is to take risk when it is appropriate.

The Choice: Cowardice or *Courage*

Let's go back to the question we asked you in the beginning of this chapter:

When you see a soldier in a movie turn and run instead of staying and fighting, what is your immediate reaction?

The movies never portray that person as a hero or someone to look up to. For most of us, our immediate reaction is to look down on that soldier as a coward. Coverage in the media of a soldier abandoning his or her post in battle is always negative. The military will charge that soldier with desertion and cowardice.

Let's look at another set of circumstances where *Courage* is tested. Answer these questions:

- *If I am in the habit of avoiding tough conversations with an employee or my boss, can I consider myself a courageous person?*
- *If I am in the habit of sidestepping issues that should be addressed in order to "keep the peace," can I consider myself a courageous person?*
- *If I never accept responsibility for my mistakes and use excuses to deflect blame, can I consider myself a courageous person?*
- *If I consistently avoid hard assignments for the sake of convenience, can I consider myself a courageous person?*
- *If I only tell the truth when I am sure doing so will not hurt me personally or financially, can I consider myself a courageous person?*

Let's just call it like it is. What is the opposite of *Courage*? Cowardice. Without *Courage*, what am I? A coward.

This is a battle every person faces. The battle between fear and our character is real. And to be a *Leader of Character*, we must win these battles. The word *coward* is never considered a compliment, and most of us don't believe cowardice is part of who we are. But if we look deeply into our decision-making processes, how often does fear win the battle versus our character?

Cowardice Versus *Courage*

Cowardice: Choosing to ignore the chronic tardiness of a high performing and tenured member of the team.
Courage: Choosing to maintain the standards for all team members no matter their tenure or job performance.

Cowardice: Choosing to allow people on your team to treat others disrespectfully.
Courage: Choosing to stop in the middle of the meeting and address a disrespectful action or comment.

Cowardice: Choosing to ignore a performance issue because of the hassles or bureaucracy involved.
Courage: Choosing to coach and to begin the documentation process early despite the hassles of HR and legal paperwork requirements.

Cowardice: Choosing to avoid confronting your boss when she is out of line or abusive towards others.
Courage: Choosing to pull your boss to the side and correct her actions even if others on the team say it is not worth it.

Cowardice: Choosing to avoid firing someone who fails to meet standards and is unwilling or unable to change.
Courage: Choosing to admit to your hiring mistake and take that person out of a job that he is unwilling or unable to do adequately.

Cowardice: Choosing to hire someone your boss likes despite your misgivings.
Courage: Choosing to specifically lay out the reasons for your concern and hold your ground unless your boss has a more convincing and adequate reason for hiring the person.

Cowardice: Choosing to complain with your peers about the decisions of your leaders without ever discussing those concerns with your leaders.

Courage: Choosing to confront your leadership with your concerns and bring alternatives to them for consideration.

The way to become courageous and avoid cowardice is to start acting courageously. We won't all have the opportunity to face an enemy who wants to kill us as our military men and women encounter. However, we all have moments that give us a choice between *Courage* and cowardice. Some of those choices may be small and others could be large. But if we truly think about it, our large choices never stand alone. The large choices we make are always influenced by the smaller day-to-day choices we made in the past. We must make the choice to overcome fear and anxiety over a perceived or actual risk and then take the appropriate action.

We need *Courage* at the moment when our *Integrity* is tested. When a friend or a boss expects us to lie for them, we must overcome the fear of losing that friend or losing our job in order to choose *Integrity* over our fear. We need *Courage* when our sense of *Duty* is challenged with a task that we are uncomfortable doing. We must overcome our fear of failure and act by choosing to do our *Duty*. As C. S. Lewis points out in the quote we shared at the start of the chapter, *Courage* is the fulcrum that is present whenever we take action and exercise our *Habits of Character*.

Courage and *Leaders of Character*

Whether you are a combat leader or a business leader. Whether you are a single parent or an unpaid leader of volunteers. *Courage* is a necessity to lead with character.

It takes *Courage* to fix bayonets and charge into the face of machine gun fire.

It takes *Courage* to challenge your boss at work when he or she is off base.

It takes *Courage* to correct the chronic tardiness of a tenured and well-respected employee.

It takes *Courage* to let your child get a "C" on a science project for his own work instead of doing it for him.

Courage is not characterized by the absence of fear, but by the willingness to take action despite that fear.

What Are We Afraid Of?

Fear is a natural part of the human condition. We all have fears and anxieties that we must face. Fear kicks in when we recognize risk. If there is a perceived or actual risk involved in an activity, fear rises up inside of us. And that fear leads us to rationalize all the reasons we should avoid taking action.

We Are Afraid of Failure

For some of us, failure seems like the worst possible outcome. The thought of screwing something up is so paralyzing that we would rather do nothing than risk taking action and be proven ineffective. While many fears seem to be part of our psyche from birth, fear of failure tends to be an acquired fear.

When we were toddlers learning to walk, we all failed and failed often. None of us started out running. As toddlers we all went through the same process of failure. One step … fall. Two steps … fall. We held onto the coffee table and took multiple steps and then fell once we let go of the table. We all failed repeatedly, and yet we never gave up! As the famous saying goes, "Failure is not an option" when toddlers are trying to walk. Pretty soon our parents were chasing us all over the house because they couldn't stop us from running.

As toddlers we truly understood that something worthwhile could create short-term failures. But we knew the failures were worth the prize of finally learning how to walk. What happened to that toddler who stared failure in the face and laughed and kept on trying? What happened to the attitude we had before our culture taught us to be afraid of failure?

To overcome the fear of failure, we must return to the days when failure was not seen as the end of the road but a pit stop on the highway to success!

To overcome the fear of failure, we must return to the days when failure was not seen as the end of the road but a pit stop on the highway to success!

We Are Afraid of Being Burned

Many people believe that time is the key ingredient to trusting others. But in reality time is not the issue. There is a fear inside many of us that prevents us from trusting others. That is the fear of getting burned. We are scared to be fooled or to be let down by someone else. Our fear may be the result of past experiences. All of us have trusted someone in the past who let us down. That experience for some of us has made us slow to trust. We have a hard time trusting others because of the pain or embarrassment we've endured in the past.

Of course, some people find it easier to trust than others do. It comes naturally to them. These people may still experience relationships that cause them hurt or disappointment, but they continue to instinctively start relationships by trusting others.

Other people are naturally slow to trust. Offering trust does not come easily to them due to their personality or upbringing.

Trust requires *Courage*. Every time I decide to trust someone, I am making myself vulnerable. I am taking a risk, whether it is a perceived or actual risk. *Courage* is the most important *Habit of Character* I must develop if I am going to build trust with the people I lead at work or at home. We can develop *Courage* by trusting people before they earn it. Being the one who trusts first takes *Courage*.

"But if I do that, won't I get burned?" Yes. You will get burned by about 20 percent of the people you have the *Courage* to trust first. So your trust will be misplaced 20 percent of the time. That also means your trust will be rightly placed 80 percent of the time! Most people want to be trusted, even those who are untrustworthy.

Here's another way to look at this. If I choose to make people earn my trust first, I am treating 20 percent of the people as they deserve to be treated and 80 percent of the people worse than they deserve. If, on the other hand, I choose to trust first, I am treating 80 percent of the people exactly as they deserve to be treated and the other 20 percent better than they deserve.

With new relationships it takes *Courage* to lead with trust. *Courage* isn't needed to distrust new people. All that is needed to distrust is fear. The question then becomes, do I choose to overcome my fear and trust people, or do I continue to have my life and my relationships controlled by fear?

We Are Afraid of Losing Relationships

Losing friendships or the loyalty of another person is the fear that prevents many of us from taking action. When we are faced with choices that can affect others or affect the perceptions others have of us, fear dominates us.

In high school and college, we call this peer pressure. Most parents warn their children, "Don't give in to peer pressure." But then those same parents head to work and do exactly what they tell their kids not to do! They bow to the peer pressure present in their job. For example, the idea of being a tattletale (or a snitch) at work prevents these parents from speaking up when something is wrong. Having a difficult conversation with an employee gets put off because it makes them uncomfortable. Speaking up for what is right in the face of a group of people never happens because they might be standing alone.

Imagine if the fear of being called a snitch did not exist. What if people just did the right thing because it was the right thing to do? Would it then be necessary for the government to give whistleblowers monetary rewards for doing the right thing?

We Are Afraid of Losing Jobs

In today's world of work pressures, family pressures, and mounting debt, the idea of losing a job can paralyze many people. The fear of telling family or friends "I lost my job" is real for many people. The fear of searching for a new position in a job market that may not be strong in your city or marketplace are fears that many people succumb to when making a choice between speaking up or stepping up at work.

When faced with these choices, we need to do some soul-searching. Ask yourself which statement you would want your children to tell their children about you, their grandparent:

"2016 was a tough year because your grandfather had the
Courage to stand up for his convictions and lost his job."

-Or-

"I am not sure what your grandfather stood for; he always did what was practical."

The lessons kids will remember and will pass on to their kids will not be about the way we kept employed by not creating waves. They will remember the way we lived. The question is, will their memories of us be memories of *Courage* or of cowardice?

We Are Afraid of the Unknown

Sometimes being unsure of what is next keeps people from acting. We cannot see around the next corner, so we stop in place and wait for more clarity. Meanwhile, the world passes us by, while those people with *Courage* round the corner and adapt to what they find. They move forward while we stand still.

Why do some people face their fears and move forward while others become the proverbial ostrich and stick their heads in the sand, wondering why their life is not going anywhere? Aristotle's answer and ours is practice. The people who move forward and overcome their fears do not have some special powers or a magic pill they take; they just have more practice in facing their fears.

The people who move forward and overcome their fears
do not have some special powers or a magic pill they
take; they just have more practice in facing their fears.

Facing Fears at West Point

Throughout the cadets' four years at the Academy, they are challenged again and again to face their fears. They faced their fear of heights and drowning by leaping off a ten-meter tower in full battledress, with a weighted backpack and a rifle. They had to touch the bottom of the pool (fifteen feet deep) and swim to the opposite side.

The women faced their fears in both a self-defense class and a close-quarters combat class (CQC). In CQC, the final exam took place in pitch-black hallways as the female cadets attacked their male classmates and were attacked by them. The men were often bigger and stronger than the women, but the women's grades were based on the same criteria as the men's were.

Every male freshman (plebe) at West Point faced his fears in boxing class. This has been the case since the early days of the physical training program at West Point. Both of us took boxing thirty years apart. Ironically, the same man, Herb Kroeten, was the lead boxing instructor for both of us. Kroeten would ask the young men in his boxing classes if any of them had ever been in a fist fight. Ninety percent of the plebes he polled during his forty-plus years as a boxing instructor had never been in a fight. Another thing every plebe boxer had in common, whether they were a good boxer or a bad one, was an overwhelming realization when they awoke in the morning that someone was going to hit them in the face that day. It was a fact that we all had to deal with every morning after reveille sounded.

The Business Guy: My Boxing Experience

The only fight I participated in prior to plebe boxing occurred on a lacrosse field in high school. The fight lasted about twenty seconds. It wasn't planned; it just happened. As a cadet in boxing class at West Point, however, I had the anticipation of fighting weighing on me all day before I climbed into the ring. It didn't matter if I had a calculus exam or an oral presentation that day. My mind was on boxing. I knew a fight was coming, and I could not avoid it. I also knew that no matter how well I boxed that day, another cadet was going to punch me in the face with all his strength. The anticipation of the fight created a totally different experience than the impromptu fight on the lacrosse field.

West Point is not a boxing school. In fact, many people might make the case that teaching boxing is unrealistic. If a young lieutenant were to get up close and personal with the enemy, it is doubtful that the civilized rules of boxing would apply. But three times a week, we climbed into the ring and learned how to box with correct form. We were trained to throw jabs, hooks, and uppercuts. We were trained to move correctly and to block our opponent's punches. But even with all that training, every other day for a semester, we knew we were going to get popped in the face.

The General: *Boxing and Combat*

Every few years I would get called to testify in Washington about the usefulness of making plebes box. Some politicians felt that boxing was an unnecessary part of the curriculum and was an outdated tradition. My response was to argue that having to climb into the ring and box every other day was probably the closest any of these young men and future officers would ever come to facing the fear they were going to face in battle. It was the best preparation available for that likely scenario.

When women entered West Point, we developed the close-quarters combat class for the same reason. Few women had ever faced the fear involved in a physical fight. The final exam required them to defend themselves against bigger and stronger attackers in a pitch-black hallway, which prepared them for the fear they would also face in future combat situations.

At the end of the semester, every plebe had three graded bouts against classmates. You were graded based on appropriate aggressiveness, boxing form, and lastly, whether you won the fight. Winning wasn't as important as how you fought. Each time you climbed into the ring, you could neither run nor lose your cool and throw undisciplined punches. You had to stick to your plan, display proper form, and not be overcome with fear or anger.

That is exactly what is expected of a young lieutenant during combat. When the first bullets begin to fly, he cannot lose his cool. He has to lead his soldiers into battle. He can't charge straight ahead without thought, nor can he run and hide. He has a plan he has to implement and adapt if things don't go exactly as the plan has anticipated. In fact, in combat things never go as planned.

Plebe boxing class and CQC followed Aristotle's beliefs that our habits form our character. As Aristotle said, you *"become just by doing just acts, … brave by doing brave acts."*

"Do the thing you are afraid to do and the death of fear is certain."
– **Ralph Waldo Emerson**

The General: *Boxing's Impact*

My doctoral research backed up both Aristotle's premise and my pro-boxing argument to the US Congress. I looked at the effects of boxing and gymnastics on the psyche of male cadets. (There were no women at West Point at the time of my research.)

In gymnastics, cadets were asked to face their fear of heights and asked to perform maneuvers that many were afraid to even try. If they did not try, they received a zero and their grade suffered.

In boxing, however, there was not a choice. Once you climbed into the ring, you could not choose not to box. You had to face your fears because you had another cadet ready to face his. If you chose not to fight, you got your clock cleaned. In boxing you had to confront your fears.

Our research found that whether a cadet did well or flunked boxing did not change what happened inside those young men. All the cadets who took boxing grew in *Courage* because they had faced their fears.

Gymnastics, on the other hand, did not have the same effect because avoiding your fears or getting a zero were viable options.

Courage is a habit. We develop it just like any other habit—one decision at a time. Just climbing into the boxing ring was the first decision for many cadets. Each time we stepped into the ring and faced our fears, we were developing *Courage*, many of us for the first time.

Two Types of *Courage*

There are really two types of *Courage*: physical *Courage* and moral *Courage*. Physical *Courage* is taking action in the face of perceived or actual physical danger. Cadets display physical *Courage* on high-dive platforms and in dark hallways and boxing rings during training. In society at large, many times we automatically call a person a hero if he or she overcomes a grave physical danger, such as a fire, robbery, car accident, or tornado. But is physical *Courage* displayed out of self-preservation on the same level with physical *Courage* on display when others are in harm's way? That is when the second type of *Courage* arises—moral *Courage*. Physical and moral *Courage* go hand in hand when someone displays physical *Courage* without regard for self. Dai Wei Minh's actions in the face of grave physical harm are a perfect example of moral and physical *Courage* coming together.

Some of the heroes who showed moral and physical *Courage* during The War on Terror by jumping on a grenade to save their friends:

- Jason Dunham (2004) – Medal of Honor (posthumous)
- Roi Klein (2006) – Medal of Honor (posthumous)
- Michael Monsoor (2006) – Medal of Honor (posthumous)
- Ross A McGinnis (2006) – Medal of Honor (posthumous)
- Kyle Carpenter (2010) – Medal of Honor

Few of us are asked to put our lives or the lives of others on the line for a cause. The physical *Courage* seen in a boxing ring, in the rice paddies of Vietnam, or the rocky mountains of Afghanistan may not apply to your situation. But moral *Courage* does apply to the *Courage* most of us need in business and in our everyday lives.

Many times we have the choice to exercise moral *Courage* when no one else knows about it. Moral *Courage* is very much a private matter between God and us. We are the only two who know our motives. When we choose *Integrity* and do the right thing, without a selfish incentive, we have acted with moral *Courage*. As C. S. Lewis stated, it is nearly impossible to truly be a person of character, to be a person of *Humility, Integrity, Duty, Selflessness, or Positivity*, without *Courage* leading the way.

We choose *Courage* over cowardice when we consistently choose to act in alignment with our beliefs no matter our circumstances or the risks involved. In other words, if we claim to believe in *Humility, Integrity, Selflessness, Duty*, and *Positivity*, then we must act courageously to actually *be* someone who can be described by these traits. That is why we have chosen to start the section on the *Habits of Character* with a discussion on *Courage*. Without *Courage*, talking about the other habits becomes no more than an academic exercise. That is not what we want for you. Our goal is to help you become a *Leader of Character*. To do that, you must demonstrate *Courage*.

Exercising *Courage*: Time to Break a Sweat

In order to build a muscle, we must exercise it. If we never push the muscle outside of it's comfort zone, it will never get stronger. *Courage* is a muscle that needs to be exercised. Some people believe that when the big tests come in life, they will be ready. They believe the *Courage* to speak up or to step up and do the right thing will be there on command. This is unrealistic. If you have never lifted fifty pounds, what makes you think you will be able to lift three hundred? It's the same with *Courage*. You need to start with small choices today that will build your *Courage* for the big tests to come. So here are some exercises you can do to establish *Courage* in your life:

Overall

- ✓ Take a stand for something you believe in but may not be popular with others.
- ✓ Tell someone when she has food in her teeth.
- ✓ Tell the truth to someone even if you don't want to rock the boat.
- ✓ Do something that makes you feel uncomfortable.
- ✓ Count the number of excuses you make each day for one week.
- ✓ Stop a friend from driving if he has been drinking.

At Work

- ✓ Talk to your boss about the demeaning way he addresses you.
- ✓ Talk to your boss about a problem she needs to address.
- ✓ Admit your weaknesses to your team or your family (by the way, they already know them).
- ✓ Talk to an employee about her inappropriate dress.
- ✓ Talk to an employee about the consequences if he does not change his behaviors.
- ✓ Stop making excuses and take responsibility for your team missing a deadline.
- ✓ Step up and take charge, even when it is inconvenient.

At Home

- ✓ Take responsibility for something that was not your fault.
- ✓ Tell your spouse or your child you are sorry and ask for forgiveness.
- ✓ Follow through on discipline you promised your children.
- ✓ Say "no" when other parents are saying "yes".
- ✓ Say "yes" when you have no real reason to say "no".
- ✓ Trust your child with a new responsibility, even if you are unsure that he or she is ready.

"Courage is not limited to the battlefield or the Indianapolis 500 or bravely catching a thief in your house. The real tests of courage are much quieter. They are the inner tests, like remaining faithful when nobody's looking, like enduring pain when the room is empty, like standing alone when you are misunderstood."

– Charles Swindoll

Chapter 5

HABIT #2: HUMILITY

The Warm-Up: Questions for Stretching Your Mind

Who is the most humble leader you know? _____

*What do they do (behaviors) that displays humility?*_____

On a scale of 1 to 10, with 10 being extremely humble, how humble are you?
_____

Rate how you think your co-workers _____, *your spouse*_____, *and your children* _____ *would rate you?*

The General's Story: *The Humility of a Four-Star General*

I first met General Creighton Abrams in 1959 when we both served in the 3rd Armored Division in Germany. He came to the division with a great reputation as a daring combat leader. We all knew about him leading his tank battalion to break through the German lines to relieve the 101st Airborne Division that was completely surrounded by German forces during the Battle of the Bulge in World War II. General George S. Patton, perhaps the greatest tank commander of all time, did not hesitate to tell other people that Abrams was the best tank commander in the Army.

We knew that General Abrams was a brilliant, highly decorated, and very demanding commander who expected everyone to do his *Duty*. As I would learn in future years, General Abrams always demonstrated the *Courage*, *Humility*, *Integrity*, and *Selflessness* that are required of a *Leader of Character*.

A decade later, in 1970, General Abrams asked me to join him in South Vietnam and to serve as his aide de camp. He had just taken command of all the American forces fighting in Vietnam. After serving closely with him in that environment, it was obvious he was a *Leader of Character* and the perfect model for anyone wanting to become such a leader.

General Abrams had done it all. He was involved in three wars and served in the turbulent peacetime years between World War II, the Korean War, and the Vietnam War. His incredible record and reputation as a brilliant commander gave him every reason to become self-centered and prideful. In fact, I met many commanders with far less to brag about who never missed a chance to promote themselves. But I have never met a person who accomplished so much yet never demonstrated even a little bit of arrogance. General Abrams was a confident yet humble leader.

When I think about a demonstration of *Humility*, I remember a trip that I made with General Abrams in Vietnam. We visited a Fire Support Base (FSB) that had been attacked during the night by a large North Vietnamese Army force. The FSB fought off the enemy the night before, and General Abrams wanted to visit the soldiers and congratulate them for the great job they did. He didn't request a formal briefing (often derisively called dog-and-pony shows) as some commanders regularly demanded. He just wanted to meet and visit the junior soldiers who did the heaviest fighting.

As we walked around the perimeter of the FSB, we stopped where a young soldier was cleaning the barrel of his machine gun. General Abrams asked the soldier, "Did your machine gun work well for you last night?"

Without looking up, the soldier replied, "Yes, Ole Betsy never lets me down. She just kept firing when ever I called on her." He was so busy cleaning "Ole Betsy" that he did not see it was a general speaking to him, let alone the four-star general in charge of everything. This FSB was located in a part of South Vietnam where the dirt is red and everything else tends to turn red. I noticed that the machine gun was red on the outside, but the soldier just kept cleaning the internal working mechanisms of "Ole Betsy." General Abrams congratulated the young soldier and told him to keep taking good care of his weapon. Then we continued on our tour.

Later, on our flight back to Saigon, General Abrams couldn't stop talking about the young soldier and "Ole Betsy." He had noticed the red clay on the outside of the machine gun, but he said he did not dare to criticize that because that young soldier was so proud of her. Here he was, a four-star Commanding General, talking about a young frontline soldier who had done his job and probably did not recognize he was talking to the guy in charge of every soldier in Vietnam. He did not even stand up and salute the Commanding General. As an officer, General Abrams would have been within his rights to demand proper military courtesy from this soldier. He could have corrected him for not adhering to the protocols established long ago for interactions between enlisted soldiers and officers. Yet General Abrams could not stop talking about that young soldier and saying how proud he was of him.

General Abrams was not concerned about whether he received the proper and well-deserved recognition for his rank and his own accomplishments. He only cared that this young soldier and "Ole Betsy" had done their *Duty* and the soldier was still alive to tell him about it. He could have chosen to be arrogant, but he chose *Humility* instead.

General Creighton Abrams, the highly decorated Commanding General in Vietnam from 1968 to 1972, was exceedingly humble in front of this young soldier. He believed and acted like "it was not about me" that day, and he was the same everyday I witnessed him in command. General Abrams was a *Leader of Character*.

The Business Guy's Story:

I knew within a week of hiring Larry that I was in trouble. I hired him because of his impressive credentials. His interviews were stellar. We had a lot in common (or so I thought) because Larry had a military background as I did. Plus, I knew

I had hired someone who was smarter than I was. This was a lesson *The General* shared with me that I embraced. He always told me to hire people smarter than I was and then trust them, and they would make me look brilliant. Of course, in my case, that is a low bar to clear!

The first clue that I had made a mistake came when my top salesperson called me and told me she had concerns about Larry. She made a suggestion to him that he immediately disregarded. A few days later I assigned Larry a mentor. Within a week that mentor called me and told me we had a problem. It turned out that Larry would not listen to his mentor either. Even though he just left the military and had never worked in sales a day in his life, Larry did not want to take any cues from other people.

Now it was my turn to work with him. I stepped in and expected that I would break through to Larry. After all, we shared a common military background, and I was bringing to him my experience in sales and sales leadership. I couldn't have been more wrong in my expectations.

I began to work with Larry on a regular basis to get him up to speed early in his career. He immediately began to complain about my presence. Every time I would point out an area for improvement, he would argue with me. In fact, it was not just a difference in opinion. He would get so angry that his face would turn bright red and a vein would begin to pop out of his forehead. The situation became so bad that I began to coach him only in public places. We would meet in hotel lobbies and in restaurants to prevent anything from escalating to the point I needed to use my plebe boxing skills.

Fortunately, it did not take long for Larry to self-destruct and lose his job. But the lesson that Larry left me with was incredibly valuable. Coachability is a window into somebody's character. If someone isn't coachable, BEWARE!

In Larry's case, and in the case of many leaders, pride prevented his growth. His unwillingness to accept that he could be wrong made him a liability instead of an asset to our team.

If a person is unable to hear constructive criticism, and he is so prideful that he believes he has no room to grow, then I do not want to work with him, let alone follow him.

Humility is the door we must pass through in order to become the *Leaders of Character* we are capable of becoming. It is the door that will lead us to the other *Habits of Character* that will prepare us and strengthen us for the character tests we will all face as leaders.

Defining *Humility*

Humility could be the least examined and most under appreciated habit we must develop to become a *Leader of Character*. The world is full of self-important, self-absorbed, and self-promoting people. The humble are rare. And they are truly a breath of fresh air when you meet them.

Unfortunately, the current culture seems to believe *Humility* is a sign of weakness. In fact, when you look at what many sources list as synonyms for *Humility*, the majority have a negative connotation. Some of the negative synonyms listed include demureness, lowliness, meekness, passivity, and unassertiveness.

Humility seems to be a virtue that is losing ground in today's world. Maybe that's because humble people do not make for good TV. The media prefers to make the bold and the brash the lead story. The self-absorbed and self-promoting are the people who make the headlines. Nightly the bravado of superstar athletes and the pride of boastful CEOs are displayed for all to see on *SportsCenter* or cable news networks. While the bravado makes for good TV ratings, the individuals strutting their stuff don't make for *Leaders of Character*.

Today, too many leaders see themselves as the center of their organizations. We have football and basketball players pounding their chest after making a play. The media follows self-made celebrities who have done nothing in their lives but build their personal brands through reality TV or social media. The music industry and Hollywood continue to find new awards shows in order to celebrate themselves.

The common denominator in all these examples is the elevation of self above others. This places the habit of *Humility* in direct conflict with these societal norms.

Andersons' 12-Word (or less) Definition of Humility
Believing and acting like "It's not about me"

Notice the verbs in this definition: *believing* and *acting*. We used both verbs because we realize some people are good at false humility. These people can say all the right things. At times they may make humble and self-deprecating comments. But do they really mean them? They play the humility game in public quite well, and then they show their true colors when they let down their guard.

Our motives are important. If I say humble things to prove my *Humility* to others, that is pride on display, not *Humility*. It is prideful because my motive is all about me. It is self-focused and meant to give *me* an advantage. The *Leader of Character*, however, truly believes and acts as if "It's not about me." Instead, such leaders honestly believe that "the world is not here for me," that "I can't go it alone," that "I am not a finished product."

To truly be a leader who stands out in today's world, *Humility* is the key. The humble leaders are often the ones who make a lasting impact. While the flash-in-the-pan, quick-fix CEO may burn bright on TV for a couple of years, the lack of substance beyond the flash soon becomes a liability. What is unique in today's culture is the humble leader, not the what's-in-it-for-me, flamboyant leader. We find it ironic that so many people today spend so much time declaring how unique they are. They want to stand out in a crowd and be noticed. Yet by doing this, they become a member of the majority, all of whom point to themselves.

Welcome to the counterculture! Can one man who was born before television (*The General*) and another who was born before cell phones (*The Business Guy*) really be countercultural? We are when we claim an essential habit of being a *Leader of Character* is *Humility*.

Here is our countercultural belief that a *Leader of Character* needs to embrace:

Humility is not a demonstration of weakness
but a quiet declaration of strength.
If you want to be a Leader of Character,
try Humility on for size.

The Business Guy: *Who's Really More Important?*

At West Point, we were humbled from Day 1. On our first day, we were herded into Eisenhower Hall Auditorium for our first class meeting. It wasn't really a meeting. The seniors in charge of Beast Barracks (Cadet Basic Training) spoke at us from a stage while we sat ramrod straight and tried not to question our sanity for volunteering for the hardships looming ahead of us over the next six weeks. During that meeting, the First Captain, the senior cadet in charge of Beast Barracks, stood in front of sixteen hundred newly sworn-in cadets and said, "I want anyone who in high school was senior class president, vice president, student body president, team captain, valedictorian, salutatorian, or eagle scout to stand up." At that moment, 80 percent of the auditorium rose to its feet. With a wry smile, the First Captain said, "Sit down. You are not the big man on campus anymore."

That was humbling, and my first realization that I was not as special as I thought I was. Which was the point. The Academy was intent on showing us that none of us in the room were more important than the next cadet. And it worked.

In dictionaries, you'll find that *confidence* is listed as an antonym to *Humility*! The world today believes that a display of confidence is more inspiring than a display of *Humility*. You might ask, "But don't people need to be confident to be noticed, let alone be seen as a leader?" Of course! There is nothing wrong with confidence. Confidence is a key attribute for successful leaders. Unfortunately, in a world where confidence is celebrated, an individual's need to proclaim his or her competence is viewed as an essential part of success. The need to be recognized by others has even been taught inside of some organizations as an essential part of getting promoted. In other words, self-aggrandizement is promoted and often confused with an accurate understanding of confidence.

Everyone wants a confident leader. But who truly wants an arrogant leader? An arrogant leader is not a *Leader of Character* and not a truly mature leader. How mature is a petulant child who needs everyone's attention? *Humility* is a sign of maturity while arrogance is a sign of immaturity.

> *"The greatest of faults is to be conscious of none."*
> **– Thomas Carlyle**

The Choice: Arrogance or *Humility*

Having both *Humility* and confidence in the same leader is rare. Nelson Mandela, Mahatma Gandhi, and Jesus Christ are three historical figures who had both. They believed in themselves and their causes. They spoke with strength and led movements that changed their societies and arguably the world as a result. Yet you rarely heard them speak about themselves. *If you did, they shared their accomplishments in a way that brought glory to others and not to themselves.* Peyton Manning and Coach Mike Krzyzewski are two examples from the world of sports today. When you hear them speak, they deflect attention towards others. If they are in the spotlight, they do everything they can to shine it on others. In each of these examples, we see a confidence that rarely, if ever, crosses the line to arrogance.

Humility is not a demonstration of weakness
but a quiet declaration of strength.

These are all people most of us would love to follow and emulate. So why do so many of us have trouble with the idea that two of the traits these men possess—confidence and *Humility*—can coexist in the same person? Maybe it is because there are so many more examples in history and in sports of confidence morphing into arrogance. This is a line many of us have crossed. We struggle when our ego takes control and confidence turns into boasting.

How can we know when we have become arrogant, when self-confidence has turned into self-promotion? Here are some indicators to consider:

- If we are more concerned about how we look to others versus what was actually accomplished, can we really claim to be humble?
- If we place ourselves at the center of the story as opposed to being just part of the story, can we claim we are humble?
- If we use a lot of adjectives to describe ourselves or our accomplishments (*best, exceptional, strongest, fastest,* or other comparative adjectives), can we claim to be humble?

We all form habits in the same way—one choice at a time. So, to become a *Leader of Character*, we have to make a choice. In this case, our choice is *not* between *Humility* or confidence. Rather, the choice we must make is between choosing *Humility* or choosing arrogance.

Arrogance Versus *Humility*

Arrogance: Choosing to fight for a strategy mainly because it was your strategy.
Humility: Choosing to compromise in order to find the best strategy instead of just your strategy.

Arrogance: Choosing to be angry with someone on your team because they made you look bad.
Humility: Choosing to take responsibility for the failure of your team, and working on a solution to fix things.

Arrogance: Choosing to stay the same person you have always been instead of trying to improve yourself.

Humility: Choosing to push yourself to change because you believe you always have room to grow, and you are committed to becoming a better version of yourself.

Arrogance: Choosing to get angry or defensive when someone within your team challenges your ideas.

Humility: Choosing to listen intently to the feedback of others, acknowledge their point of view, and make changes when they are warranted.

Arrogance: Choosing to end a conversation with the other person knowing more about you than you know about them.

Humility: Choosing to ask more questions and listen longer than the other person does.

If I cannot honestly claim to be humble, then I am probably arrogant. Those two traits are at odds with each other. But *Humility* and confidence can go hand in hand. They are not mutually exclusive. Quarterback Peyton Manning talks more about the teammates who helped him break multiple NFL records, and he routinely picks defenses apart with his quarterbacking skills. Ghandi was an incredibly humble leader who had the confidence to take on the British Empire. Jesus Christ stood quietly in front of his taunters and accusers, yet he had the confidence to call the religious leaders of his day hypocrites and a brood of vipers.

Confidence with *Humility*

That first year at West Point is a humbling experience for most cadets. The majority of cadets are an academic, athletic, or leadership standout in high school. Many are all three. The *Humility* that comes through learning to follow as a plebe is a critical building block for developing *Leaders of Character* at West Point.

However, after a humbling plebe year, *Humility* was rarely a topic covered as a key leadership trait. It was not part of the curriculum or even something many instructors at the Academy delved into informally. Welcome again to the counterculture in leadership development. *Humility* is so countercultural that even the most prestigious leadership school in the United States does not officially discuss *Humility* in its character curriculum. *Humility* is the one hole we believe West Point needs to address.

After breaking down the arrogance of the high school seniors during our freshman year, the next three years focused on building us up into young men and women who truly believed we could accomplish anything. We were meant to be confident young officers, but many of us became prideful to a fault. West Point did a great job instilling confidence in us, but it did little after that first year to temper that confidence with *Humility*. Some individuals came to West Point already believing "It's not about me." Others learned that lesson while we were cadets. Some of us, however, had to learn *Humility* through adversity after graduation.

Not everyone learns the lesson. Young Academy graduates have a reputation for overwhelming confidence that can cross the line to arrogance. Whether it was during field operations or in the officers' clubs, the egos of many graduates became legendary. Our ROTC counterparts and the women we met at the Officers' Club can vouch for this observation.

Fortunately, the Army and God tended to handle our arrogance later in life. As the years go on in the Army, the confidence that crossed the threshold to arrogance often dissipated. The challenges we faced in the military had a way of humbling many of us. If the military failed to accomplish this, God often takes care of it in other areas of our lives.

Though West Point may not include *Humility* in it's curriculum, West Point frequently produces leaders who develop *Humility* before, during, or after graduation. These graduates truly believe "It's not about me." They are competent, confident, and humble. They are the *Leaders of Character* West Point's Purpose Statement proclaims as the institution's ultimate goal.

Humility is not synonymous with lack of confidence. On the contrary, we believe that *Humility* is actually a display of confidence. When we do not need to beat our own chests and market ourselves to those around us, when we quietly do our jobs well and seek the welfare of others over ourselves, we exhibit real confidence. We can be humble and confident simultaneously.

Arrogance and *Humility*, on the other hand, are always in opposition. While an arrogant person is usually preoccupied with promoting her capabilities, a confident person does not need other people to know she is capable.

Humility is not synonymous with passivity either. No one would ever consider Mandela, Ghandi, Jesus, Peyton Manning, or Coach K passive leaders. They did not let people walk all over them. The strength of their convictions and belief in their abilities made them leaders of action.

Confidence is a strength, and so is *Humility*. When they are paired in the same person, we are blessed by that person's presence in our lives. Like many things that are rare, this combination is a valuable commodity.

Confidence tempered with *Humility* should be a *Leader of Character's* goal.

Humility and *Leaders of Character*

Many seemingly arrogant leaders are actually insecure leaders. That insecurity comes from putting too much focus on themselves. "What do others think about *me*? What if *my* team doesn't perform well? What will people think of me then? *My* reputation is at stake!" Whether someone displays his self-centeredness as insecurity or as arrogance, the source is still pride. Self-focused comments and the attitude undergirding them put the individual in the center of the story. When we put ourselves at the center, it often prevents us from admitting mistakes or sharing our weaknesses with others. These are not the marks of leaders who inspire followers.

Leaders of Character Say, "I blew it!"

It takes *Humility* to admit when you blew it. The humble do not see the need to be perfect because they already know perfection is impossible. They see themselves realistically, as flawed human beings. Therefore, admitting mistakes does not damage their self-image. A *Leader of Character* does not see his mistakes as a sign of weakness but as a sign of humanity. He admits his mistakes to his superiors, his peers, his employees, and his family.

A *Leader of Character* does not see his mistakes
as a sign of weakness but as a sign of humanity.

As *Leaders of Character*, we must ask ourselves:

"When was the last time I publicly admitted to my mistakes?"

The *Leader of Character* is secure enough to say, "It's my fault. Please forgive me." The arrogant leader may never say those words, because his pride won't allow him to.

Leaders of Character Say, "I need help!"

A *Leader of Character* is also secure enough to know she has weaknesses. She knows she should gain wisdom from other people. She actively seeks new information and advice from wise counselors. And whether the wisdom comes from a respected authority figure or a frontline employee, the *Leader of Character* is open to wise counsel no matter what title someone else holds. *Humility* allows a leader to see the worth of the wisdom independent of the one who gave it.

The arrogant leader, however, may ask for the opinions of others, but such a leader rarely implements or even seriously considers another person's ideas or solutions. Instead, this kind of person is looking for accolades, flattery, and anything else that will boost her ego. She's not after wisdom—at least not a wisdom found outside of herself.

A *Leader of Character* is secure enough to ask for the opinions of others and truly make changes based on the feedback of others. She knows that without the wisdom of others, she is likely to stagnate and fail as a leader.

As *Leaders of Character*, then, we must ask ourselves:

"When was the last time I accepted advice from someone else?"

Without the *Humility* to admit mistakes or weaknesses, we will never grow to be the *Leader of Character* we are capable of becoming. We need the input of others to grow as leaders and to lead well. Furthermore, our reluctance to accept responsibility and deflect blame to someone or some circumstance gives us no reason to grow. Without the safety net of an excuse, we automatically become problem-solvers instead of blame shifters. This is critical for *Leaders of Character* to grow.

> Without the safety net of an excuse, we automatically become problem-solvers instead of blame shifters.

Leaders of Character Say, "I am listening"

A *Leader of Character* demonstrates *Humility* by being a good listener. He is comfortable being quiet and not always having center stage or getting in the last word. He listens longer and asks more questions than others. *Humility* makes the *Leader of Character* very comfortable learning about others and demonstrating the lost art of listening. He does not always dominate the conversation with stories about his own accomplishments or those of his children.

The *Leader of Character* tends to make others feel important instead of making himself feel that way. He does that by listening. Listening may be one of the best ways to let others know you care about them more than you care about yourself.

Many times we may claim to be listening to others, but more often than not we are just preparing to make our own arguments or tell our own stories. As *Leaders of Character*, we must ask ourselves:

"Am I really listening to others, or am I just waiting to talk?"

We want to be clear here. *Being selfless doesn't mean you think less of yourself. It just means you think of yourself less.* The humble put others before themselves. In Chapter 7 we will unpack the selfless art of listening in more detail. In the meantime, we want you to catch our key point here: *Humility* is a critical component of *Selflessness*. The willingness of a *Leader of Character* to listen and put others before himself starts with him acting and believing that "It is not about me."

Leaders of Character Say, "I always have room to grow"

One of the true marks of a humble leader is that he is not the same leader he was twelve months ago. The arrogant leader is stagnant. His way of leading does not change. Some people even boast about not changing their style or methods. *Leaders of Character*, however, are constantly looking to get better and grow—because they know they need it. In the end, the arrogant leader gets left behind because the *Leaders of Character* are secure enough to believe they still have a lot to learn and truly want to get better at their craft.

So, as *Leaders of Character* we must ask ourselves:

"What have I done to become a better version of myself in the last twelve months?"

If we see a leader who can openly own his mistakes and weaknesses, who truly listens to others and is on a consistent pursuit to become a better leader and a better person, who among us wouldn't follow him to hell and back? *Leaders of Character* are people we want to follow and emulate. They inspire us to be better than we would be without them in our lives.

If we see a leader who can openly own his mistakes and weaknesses, who truly listens to others and is on a consistent pursuit to become a better leader and a better person, who among us wouldn't follow him to hell and back?

Consider the billions of dollars spent by individuals and organizations on books and seminars focused on topics such as trust, team building, coaching, communications, and the like. Why have these resources been largely ineffective? One critical reason can often be traced back to the pride of the leaders they were meant to help. Prideful leaders tend to refuse to admit mistakes, weaknesses, or a need for growth. They don't listen to others because they don't see the necessity, or they believe they have more important things to do. Leaders such as this don't need to be presented with better strategies for team building or coaching, or with skills to enhance communication or human resource development. Leaders drowning in their own self-promotion, arrogance, and insecurities need a change of character—their own! Without that, nothing else will have any significant impact. Problems will remain, and solutions will be elusive.

To counter pride, we need *Humility*. And *Humility* is a foundational *Habit of Character* that makes the habits of *Duty, Selflessness,* and *Positivity* character strengths for a *Leader of Character*. Just like *Courage, Humility* is critical to treating the disease that hinders the development of *Leaders of Character*. We must exercise and build this muscle to have strong enough character to lead our teams, our families, and our countries.

> *"To be successful you must be interested in finding the best way, not in having your way."*
> – **Coach John Wooden**

Exercising *Humility*: Time to Break a Sweat

The humble *Leaders of Character* are the countercultural revolutionaries we should rally behind because they are not concerned about their position. They are not obsessed with getting the spotlight. Instead they *believe* and *act* like "It's not about me."

If we told you we wanted you to meet a unique person who was confident, able to admit mistakes, a good listener, and mature enough to admit he or she had room to grow, would you want to meet such a person? Wouldn't you want to spend time with that individual? Doesn't that sound like someone we would all want to follow? To become such a person, we must make the daily choice to be humble.

These small exercises in *Humility* that follow will help you build the *Habit of Character* we define as *Humility*. It is a muscle that needs to be exercised to prepare us to defeat our arrogance or insecurity when we get tested. The big tests are coming! Will your character be in shape and ready?

Overall

- ✓ Listen twice as much as you speak.
- ✓ Don't talk about yourself unless specifically asked. Make the other person the center of the conversation.
- ✓ Find a mentor and ask him to push you outside your comfort zone.
- ✓ Call your waiter or waitress by their name. Ask for it if they do not offer it.
- ✓ Serve a meal at a homeless shelter.
- ✓ Return your grocery cart to the stack versus leaving it for the attendant to handle.
- ✓ Do something for someone without expecting anything in return.
- ✓ Pick up trash on the sidewalk that others are walking by.
- ✓ Open a door for others whether they are young or old, male or female.
- ✓ After your flight is cancelled, let someone else go before you at the airline ticket counter.
- ✓ Give money anonymously to a church or charity no matter how big or small the gift is.
- ✓ Don't fight to win an argument. Fight to solve the problem.
- ✓ Park at the far end of the parking lot, leaving the closer spaces for other people.
- ✓ Give up your seat to another person on the subway or train.
- ✓ Do something beneficial without someone asking you to, and don't tell anyone about it.
- ✓ Greet or speak to each person you encounter in the hallway, at the gas station, at the store … you get the idea.

At Work

- ✓ Ask an employee to teach you more about her job.
- ✓ Don't worry about who gets credit for anything anymore.
- ✓ Give credit to others and avoid "I" when discussing accomplishments.
- ✓ Ask your peers or employees for one thing they would change about you. Then don't argue, and work on changing.
- ✓ Admit to a supervisor, peer, or employee when you are wrong.

At Home

- ✓ Ask your spouse or children for one thing they would change about you, then don't argue with them, just start working on changing.
- ✓ Ask for forgiveness from your spouse or from your children.
- ✓ Ask your children to show you how to use a new App.
- ✓ Do a task at home that someone else usually does.

PART 3

THE FINAL
FOUR HABITS

Introduction

HOW EACH HABIT
STRENGTHENS THE OTHER

The hierarchy for our *Habits of Character* is simple. *Courage* and *Humility* are paramount to developing the other *Habits of Character*. Without them, *Integrity, Selflessness, Duty,* and *Positivity* may come and go from our lives depending on our circumstances. This is the counterculture nature of our workout plan. We can't act like *Leaders of Character* based on our circumstances. We must consistently choose *Integrity, Selflessness, Duty,* and *Positivity* no matter our current situation. It takes both *Courage* and *Humility* to make those choices.

The four *Habits of Character* we unpack in Part 3 depend on *Courage* and *Humility* but are interrelated as well. You will see this as we define each habit and discuss the choices each one requires of us. These four do not stand alone from the other two or from each other. Like the redwood trees in the forests of Northern California, whose roots are intertwined and strengthen the trees next to them, *Integrity, Selflessness, Duty,* and *Positivity* work together to strengthen our character as well. An exercise that builds the habit of *Duty* may strengthen our habit of *Integrity* and vice versa. Another exercise that builds up the *Selflessness* muscle will develop our habit of *Positivity* as well. Part 3 breaks down each of these individual *Habits of Character*, while also strengthening the other habits around it. As each of our *Habits of Character* grow in strength, our overall character is strengthened. Even though doing push-ups strengthen our chest muscles, they also affect our triceps, shoulders, and back. This is a workout plan that will leave few areas untouched during your daily character workout. It will therefore prepare you for the larger character challenges you will face as a leader.

Chapter 6

HABIT #3: INTEGRITY

The Warm-Up: Questions for Stretching Your Mind

Who do you know that has the highest Integrity? _____

How do you define Integrity? _____

_____

Do you consider yourself to be a person of Integrity? _____

The General's Story: *Retrieving the Bodies of the Fallen*

When I assumed command of my battalion in Vietnam in January 1970, I told the soldiers that I could not promise them that they would not die in Vietnam. However, I said I would make a commitment to them: if they did die, I would use everything within my authority to assure that their bodies would be recovered and sent home to their loved ones for a decent burial. I maintain that a violation of such a commitment would be a violation of my *Integrity*.

In May 1970 while commanding that battalion, I found that my *Integrity* was tested. We were part of a larger military force sent into Cambodia to discover, capture, and destroy weapons and food items that were hidden in cache sites along the South Vietnamese border. The North Vietnamese were preparing for an attack into South Vietnam to overthrow the government.

On May 3rd, our battalion conducted an air-mobile assault into Cambodia, near the town of Snoul. We captured tons of weapons, ammunitions, explosives, and rice that were in a cache referred to as "The City."

The battalion was then assigned to another Area of Operation (AO) and established a new fire support base (FSB) called FSB DAVID. We had four rifle companies and one headquarters company. Each of the rifle companies was assigned their own AO and given the mission to conduct thorough searches of their AO.

On one of those searches, the Delta Company commander sent out a sixteen-man reconnaissance patrol to locate a rumored cache site. While searching for the site, the patrol walked into an enemy bunker complex of about twenty bunkers and got caught in a vicious crossfire. The patrol leader did an excellent job getting the patrol out of the bunker complex, and the company was successful in recovering and evacuating fourteen wounded patrol members. I was also notified by the company commander that we had two soldiers dead and missing. I gave him the mission of taking the company back to the bunker complex, destroying it, and recovering the bodies of our two dead soldiers. He replied, "WILCO," which means "will comply."

At the next day's staff meeting, I asked how Delta Company was doing in recovering our two dead soldiers. Since no one had an answer, I asked the communications officer to set up a secure radio link with the Delta Company commander. On that call he told me they were unable to accomplish the mission because the men refused to go back into the bunker complex. I told the company commander to pop a yellow smoke grenade at first light because I was coming out to speak with him and his company.

The next morning a helicopter took me, the Command Sergeant Major, and another company commander to Delta Company's location. The helicopter could not land because of the dense jungle, so we rappelled to the ground through the forest canopy.

I asked the Command Sergeant Major to talk with the enlisted soldiers while I spoke with the officers. First, I spoke with the company commander, and I asked him what he had done and said in order to get his soldiers to follow him to retrieve the bodies of our two dead soldiers.

He said to me, "Sir, it wasn't quite like that. I decided that I could not lead these men back into the bunker complex because I did not want to risk anymore lives in order to recover two dead bodies."

I asked him, "Are you telling me, here and now, that you refuse to lead this company to recover the bodies of our two dead soldiers?"

"Sir, I cannot risk anymore lives to get two dead bodies," he responded. "I do not want it on my conscience." At that point, I relieved him of his command and called for the company commander who was waiting in the helicopter to "come on down."

When I asked the Command Sergeant Major how he felt about the attitudes of the enlisted men, he told me, "The soldiers are ready to go. All they need is someone to lead them."

Then the three platoon leaders came to me and said, "Sir, if you relieve the company commander, we request that you relieve us also because we were a party to the decision that we should not risk anymore lives to recover two dead bodies."

"That decision was not for the company commander to question," I replied. "When I took command of this battalion, I made a commitment to everyone in this battalion that if you died on the battlefield here in Vietnam, I would do everything within my authority to make certain that your body was recovered and sent home to your loved ones for a decent burial. That was my decision to make, and it was his job to carry out the mission." I then told the platoon leaders to return to their platoons and get them ready because we were going back into that bunker complex and recover our two dead soldiers.

A little while later, one of the platoon leaders came up to me and said, "Sir, this isn't going to work, because I can't find anyone in my platoon who will volunteer to walk the point." (The first soldier in line as a unit moves toward the enemy.)

I said to him, "Since when is the point man a job for a volunteer? It should be one of your best soldiers. I will be the point man. We are going in there and find the bodies of our soldiers. Now get your platoon ready to move out!"

Right before the order came to move out, the platoon sergeant of the lead platoon came up to me and said, "Colonel, you do not belong up here. I have a good soldier and he has been the point man a number of times. He will do a good job."

"Alright," I replied, "then I will be behind the first squad."

We called in the air strikes and long-range artillery as we approached the bunkers in an assault line. During the short firefight, we took out each of the bunkers and found our two soldiers inside of one of them. They had been stripped of their boots and clothing. We cleared out an area where a helicopter could land, and it flew them to an aid station so they could be sent home to their families for burial.

As we got reorganized and began moving away from the objective area, we took a check on our casualties. We had two minor ones. During the assault, the Command Sergeant Major was just to my right front. A round hit the barrel of his weapon, a small piece of shrapnel hit him in the forearm, and a piece of that shrapnel hit me in the shoulder. We sustained minor wounds that were treated with A&D® Ointment and bandages.

I knew that if we walked away without making any effort to recover those soldiers, my *Integrity* might be questioned. If I asked other soldiers to do something dangerous in the future, what would they do? Would they trust me or my decisions? In combat, if soldiers don't trust their leaders, people die.

I felt that it was my responsibility to accompany those soldiers back into the bunkers to recover the bodies of our dead soldiers. After all, I was the one who made the commitment to all of my soldiers. I felt a responsibility to help do what was necessary to send those soldiers home to their families. My *Integrity* is in my control. *Integrity* can be easy to lose and hard to regain. I was not going to go back on my word to my soldiers because one of my company commanders refused to fulfill his moral obligation to lead his men.

The Business Guy's Story: *The Gentleman's Club*

If anyone has been in a large organization conducting a national strategy or training meeting, you may be familiar with the following scenario.

The day started at 7:30 a.m. Ten hours later, after speakers, marketing presentations, and training workshops, there was a herd of hungry sales people who just spent the whole day sitting when most of their days were spent moving, talking, laughing, and interacting. After such a long day, I often found myself part of a familiar ritual. I would be part of a group of guys standing in the hotel lobby trying to figure out what to do for dinner. Invariably, someone would suggest going to a gentleman's club. That did not happen at all sales conventions, but it happened enough that I knew what to expect when I went along with the crowd. Suffice it to say, those clubs are not truly for gentlemen. At a certain point in my life, I decided I was not going to join the guys on these excursions anymore.

Well, the next time I found myself in a hotel lobby discussing dinner options, my new resolve was tested. Someone suggested a gentleman's club in the host city. At that point, I made a choice that I had not made before. I told the guys I wasn't going along. After a few puzzled looks and some shrugging of shoulders, I went back to my room and ordered room service.

When I returned home, I met with a mentor of mine and proudly told him the story. Expecting a lot of affirmations and pats on the back, I was surprised when he asked me, "Why didn't you tell those guys why you weren't going to the strip club?" The conversation that I thought was going to be full of "Way to go, Dave!" became another soul-searching discipling session. Why hadn't I spoken up? Why did I quietly go to my room thankful no one asked me why I wasn't going along? The answer was fear. I was scared of their reaction, and I was scared of losing my friends.

Six months later, at another sales meeting, I had another shot. When someone suggested we should go to a strip club for dinner, I again said I wasn't going to go with the group. That is when peer pressure kicked in.

"Come on, Dave! We hardly see each other anymore."

"You have always gone before!"

"What's the deal man? Remember how much fun we had in … ?"

At that point I took a critical step that has impacted my life for decades now. With conviction and confidence that could only have been divinely inspired (because I was tremendously apprehensive about sounding hypocritical or self-righteous and losing friends), I said, "Guys, I am not going tonight because it is dishonoring to my wife and to my God."

There was a long silence among the group. The silence was broken by one of the men who asked, "What are you going to do then, Dave?"

"Well, I thought I'd go to the sports bar in the hotel, eat some wings, and watch the Duke-North Carolina game.

"You want some company? I'll go with you." Three of the guys in the group joined me at the sports bar. The rest of the men left the hotel, sticking to their original plans.

I always knew I was making a bad choice when I followed or led other men to those clubs. But I had made a good first step in a different direction when I chose to quietly stay alone at the hotel that first time. And now that I had spoken up and said why I was making the choice to stay away from those clubs, I knew I had truly fulfilled my potential to act as a true man of *Integrity*. I wished it had not taken me until my thirties to realize I was failing these tests of my *Integrity*. But I am thankful for the mentoring of a good friend and the *Courage* the Lord gave me at the moment I was tested.

The key to making those choices when my *Integrity* was challenged was *Courage*. I needed the *Courage* to act based on what I knew to be right and to speak up for what I knew was the right thing to do. Even more importantly, with this act of *Integrity*, I was also making a choice that strengthened other *Habits of Character* I needed to exercise—namely, *Duty* and *Selflessness*.

> "Right is right, even if everyone is against it; and wrong is wrong, even if everyone is for it."
>
> **– William Penn**

Defining *Integrity*

So what is *Integrity*? Like the other terms we have discussed, if we asked a room full of people to write down their understanding of *Integrity*, very few would have the same response. We must define what we stand for before we can claim it to be one of our values.

Andersons' 12-Word (or less) Definition of Integrity
Doing what is good, right, and proper, even at personal cost

Common synonyms for *Integrity*: honesty, purity, sincerity,
candor, virtue, goodness, incorruptibility, righteousness

You may remember integers in math class. They are whole numbers, such as one, two, and three. The word *integrity* comes from the Greek word *integer* meaning "whole or pure." So *Integrity*, then, carries the root meaning of wholeness, purity. In other words, part-time *Integrity* or *Integrity* when it is convenient does not meet this standard of wholeness or purity.

So if I claim to be a person of *Integrity*, is that really true if I only act with *Integrity* when I have nothing to lose? If I only do the right thing when it's easy? That's not *Integrity*; that's pragmatism.

There is nothing whole or pure when I only tell the truth 70 percent of the time, or I only do what is right when it is not risky. Being a person of *Integrity* is hard! And none of us exhibit it perfectly. There has been just one person who ever walked this earth who always thought, spoke, and acted with *Integrity*. And as much as he drew people to himself and what he taught, those who could not handle him executed him on a cross. *Integrity* comes with risk. Of course, to live without *Integrity* carries risk too—the risk of being found out as a liar, a fraud, a deceiver, a person who looks out for number one first and always.

To be a person of *Integrity*, we must strive for that purity or wholeness that is the root of the word. It is a struggle we all must actively engage in if we want to be a *Leader of Character* for the people who follow us at work and the families who love us at home.

Now, *Integrity* goes beyond mere honesty. Many people equate honesty with *Integrity*. It's true that honesty is a component of *Integrity*. Honesty, or truth-telling, is a good and honorable habit to have as long as we have proper motives. Many times people will claim, "I am just being honest!" when they are doing something out of self-interest. There is a motive component to *Integrity* that we need to consider. When we speak, are we saying something truthful that is also hurtful—all in an attempt to get ahead or get our way? Honest speech does not always come with pure motives. In other words, we need to ask ourselves, "Am I trying to help improve the situation or the other person? Or do I have selfish or other impure motives for speaking honestly?" A person with *Integrity* speaks the truth in a way that upholds others and seeks to improve the situation for others. Selfishness is not at work.

Take as an example the corporate whistleblower who exposes a company for unethical business practices that actually break federal laws. The United States federal government has incentives in place to encourage whistleblowers to step forward. A whistleblower can receive up to 10 to 30 percent of the fines paid by an employer for an SEC violation. The False Claims Act allows whistleblowers to receive 15 to 25 percent of the fines paid. Some companies are now paying fines that reach into the billions of dollars. Two famous cases awarded the whistleblowers $102 million and $104 million respectively. That is an amazing payout for someone who makes the choice to do the right thing.

Here is a question to consider: Is it truly an act of *Integrity* if the whistleblower's primary motive for doing the right thing is the monetary reward he will receive? We are not arguing against rewarding or protecting whistleblowers. They are often going out on a limb to expose illicit practices. But if a whistleblower is acting primarily for monetary benefit, should we think of him as a bastion of *Integrity*?

We are also not encouraging judging another person's motives. We think that's a bad practice. Most of the time, we are the only people who truly know our motives. And in the case of exposing corporate crime, the only person who knows the true motives of the whistleblower is the whistleblower himself.

Still, if someone has impure motives for doing the right thing, should that be considered an act of *Integrity*? Is it truly an act of *Integrity* if the motives of the individual originated from a place of self-interest? We don't think so. Motives matter. Acts of *Integrity* are not self-centered acts. They are not inspired by monetary gain. They flow from something deeper, something better, something that's morally whole, not morally complicit.

Unethical Rule Followers

At West Point, as in many organizations, there are rules and regulations people must follow. But what West Point realizes and that many organizations fail to consider is that we can all be unethical rule followers. Just because we do not break the law or a corporate regulation does not make us a person of *Integrity*.

West Point teaches the "Three Rules of Thumb" that are meant to guide cadets and officers toward wise and honorable decisions. Because every decision we make in life will not be specifically covered by rules, regulations, or laws, these "Three Rules of Thumb" can help all of us as we evaluate our motives prior to taking action.

1. Does this action attempt to deceive anyone or allow anyone to be deceived?
2. Does this action allow the gain of privilege or advantage to which I or someone else would not otherwise be entitled?
3. Would I be satisfied with the outcome if I were on the receiving end of this action?

As we examine our decisions through the lens of the "Three Rules of Thumb," it becomes clear that *Integrity* goes beyond just knowing the rules and following them. We need to consider if deception or gaining an undeserved advantage might be involved. *Integrity* also goes beyond just doing the right thing, for we can do what is right for the wrong reasons. *Integrity* goes to a different level, a deeper one, when we understand that it includes the motives that undergird our actions. We must consider our choices carefully.

The Choice: Hypocrisy or *Integrity*

What we do and why we do it matters. And when what we should do is not spelled out in black and white, what we choose to do will reveal whether we are persons of *Integrity* or something else.

Do I speak up and get fired? Or do I stay quiet and sacrifice my *Integrity*?

Do I stop my best friend from cheating on a test and lose her as a friend? Or do I stay quiet and sacrifice my *Integrity*?

What we choose to do will show others—and ourselves—who we really are.

Lying and Being a Liar

Someone who claims to believe one thing yet does another is a hypocrite. That is what I am if my actions do not follow my beliefs or my words. Another word for this is *liar*!

Let's not candy-coat anything to make ourselves feel better. Right here and right now, we are throwing out the euphemisms that attempt to make our lack of *Integrity* sound less consequential. Here are some of these:

- "A white lie"—telling one makes me a *liar*.
- "A fib"—this also makes me a *liar*.
- "A half-truth"—makes me a *liar*.
- "A strategic omission of information"—this too makes me a *liar*.

These and many other euphemisms are what we use to make ourselves feel better about being liars. If we believe we are truly persons of *Integrity* yet consistently lie, we are hypocrites. End of story, no excuses.

Hypocrisy Versus *Integrity*

Hypocrisy: Choosing to tell someone you are five minutes away when you know it will likely take longer for you to arrive.

Integrity: Choosing to admit you left home late, to ask for forgiveness, and to give a realistic timeline.

Hypocrisy: Choosing to promise to have a project completed by a certain date knowing that date is unlikely.

Integrity: Choosing to state that the date is a best-case scenario and giving a realistic date for full completion.

Hypocrisy: Choosing to allow members on your team to work together on a corporate mandated compliance or product knowledge test.

Integrity: Choosing to set clear testing guidelines and expectations, even if your team is the only one doing it.

Hypocrisy: Choosing to do your son's science project for him even after teaching him honesty since he was able to talk.

Integrity: Choosing to allow your son to get a lower grade based on his own work.

Hypocrisy: Choosing to do nothing as your supervisor makes decisions that are at least unethical and potentially illegal because you fear for your job.

Integrity: Choosing to challenge your boss to make changes and reporting her to the proper people if she does not.

Hypocrisy: Choosing to blame circumstances or others for your failure to finish a project you procrastinated doing for your spouse.

Integrity: Choosing to ask for forgiveness for not following through on your promises.

Hypocrisy: Choosing to give begrudgingly to a charity to impress customers, a girlfriend, a boyfriend, or anyone else.

Integrity: Choosing to give generously to charities you truly believe in.

When we have the *Courage* to look in the mirror and call a spade a spade when it comes to our *Integrity*, it makes it hard to justify sacrificing our *Integrity*. Choosing to become a person of *Integrity* is hard. Acting with *Integrity* will create choices for us that we may not want, which is yet another reason why it is a *Habit of Character* we must develop. *Integrity* cannot be a part-time choice. We must commit ourselves to it and live it out consistently. You have to DO what you want to BE!

Integrity and *Leaders of Character*

"If doing the right thing were easy, everyone would be doing it!"
– The General

Leaders of Character have *Integrity* because they have the *Courage* to stand up for what is right, even if it costs them personally. They go beyond knowing what to do in a tough situation. They exercise the *Courage* to take action and then proclaim why they acted.

We believe that there are three steps to acting with *Integrity*: know, do, and say.

1. Know: discern right from wrong
2. Do: take action, even at personal cost
3. Say: tell why you took action

Let's take a closer look at each of these steps.

Step 1: Know—Discern Right from Wrong

The first step is figuring out what is the right thing to do. This is easier than many people make it today. Inside every one of us, our Creator has implanted a deep-seated knowledge of what is right and what is wrong. This is very easy to see in daycare centers everywhere. No matter the religious affiliation of the parents or the exposure to cultural ideas of right and wrong, every child knows it is wrong when another child takes away her toy or strikes her without provocation. Very few people will deny that, somewhere deep inside of them, they have a voice that tells them when something is not right. We may have become effective at suppressing that voice; our base instincts, our sinful natures, work hard to push it down, to silence it. But each of us knows that voice is there. The more you access that voice, the more likely you are to hear it. The more you ignore it, the fainter it becomes. It is inside all of us. Christians call it the Holy Spirit. Others may call it conscience. Whatever you call it, that small voice is in there trying to get your attention.

Beyond what we are born with, we have the lessons of right and wrong taught in families, schools, churches, and other social and religious groups across the world. All of these groups promote a similar version of right and wrong, at least the most basic ethical principles and practices. For example, lying and cheating are frowned upon, and acting in the interest of others is commended. Caring for babies rather than slaughtering them or abusing them is upheld as right.

Our internal moral compass joined to our upbringing are the reasons we read news reports from Beijing, Moscow, Capetown, Brazilia, Chicago, or Dallas that communicate outrage when the media discovers a leader who has lied or cheated or when a passenger on a sinking ship pushes past an elderly woman to get on a lifeboat.

Knowing right from wrong is a critical step to becoming a man or woman of *Integrity*, but it is also the easiest. Unfortunately, too many people believe they are a person of *Integrity* because they can describe the right things to do in many situations. *Integrity* is not just knowing what to do. As we've discussed, to truly be a person of *Integrity*, we have to put what we know into action. Action takes *Integrity* from an intellectual exercise to a behavioral habit—a *Habit of Character.*

Step 2: Do—Take Action, Even at Personal Cost

"Here lies Dave Anderson. He did the right thing when it wasn't risky."

Who cares if we know the right thing to do and then never make the choice to do the right thing! There is no *Integrity* without action. In order for *Integrity* to become part of our character, we must choose to act with *Integrity* on a consistent basis.

Also, who cares if we know the right thing to do and then only choose to do the right thing when it won't hurt us personally! We cannot claim to be a person of *Integrity* when we only do what is right when there is no risk involved. Am I willing to endure inconvenience, discomfort, or even pain for the sake of my *Integrity*? Are you? This is why it takes *Courage* to have *Integrity.* Without *Courage*, all our claims to *Integrity* or *Duty* or *Selflessness* ring hollow.

Our *Integrity* is one of the few things in our lives we have control over 100 percent of the time. We complain about the weather, other people, the government, the media, and a lot of other things that are out of our control. We expend much time and energy on these matters, and we can rarely change them. Yet when it comes to our *Integrity*, many of us will give it up in a heartbeat just to make our life a little easier. Exercising *Integrity* may sometimes make our lives uncomfortable for a while. We may even lose a friend, take a monetary loss, or even forfeit a job. But if we can look at ourselves in the mirror and our children in the eye and tell them why we are no longer friends with a certain family or why we are changing jobs, then we have taught them a life lesson that will last into adulthood.

Take a second to do the tombstone test. Which would you rather have your kids put on your tombstone?

"Here lies <u>Your Name</u>. He did the right thing when it wasn't risky."

Or

"Here lies <u>Your Name</u>, a person of Integrity."

To have *Integrity*, we must take action. We must be willing to fight our instinct for self-preservation and our desire for comfort in order to truly have *Integrity*. The easy path is rarely the path to character. It is also the road less travelled and the road that will lead us to a life that will be remembered for its *Integrity*.

Step 3: Say—Tell Why You Took Action

Silent *Integrity* does not go far enough. Look at what happened when *The Business Guy* spoke up and said why he was not joining the group at the gentleman's club for dinner. (A gentleman's club for dinner? Is that why men go—for the food? Isn't this really a lie wrapped up in a euphemism?) When *The Business Guy* spoke up, three other men joined him in the hotel sports bar to watch a great basketball game. Would they have done that if *The Business Guy* had remained silent? Likely not, but we can't be sure. One thing we do know is that something changed the moment someone had the *Courage* to say why he was making a different choice.

What would have happened if someone at the highest levels of Enron, or some member of Bernie Madoff's team, or an individual in FIFA had spoken up about what was going on? Surely there were people in those organizations who knew bad things were happening. But people chose to remain quiet, to not get involved. They chose to protect themselves rather than do the right thing and speak up for it. What if someone had chosen to speak out earlier? Would Enron have been able to go so far that the whole company collapsed with thousands of employees losing their life savings? Would Bernie Madoff have been able to steal from so many people and lose millions of their dollars with no chance of recovering those funds? Would FIFA's host countries and their populations be burdened with multiple, multi-million dollar stadiums that went grossly over-budget and today go underused?

Knowing what to do and remaining silent about it is not enough. Choosing to do the right thing, even if it costs you personally, is the next step and that is often hard to do. But to speak up for what is right after you have personally acted with *Integrity* takes *Courage* and is the ultimate measure of *Integrity*. Granted, this is a high bar to clear. Neither *The General* nor *The Business Guy* have always been the leader, husband, or men we are called to be because we failed to clear that bar. Doing the right thing is not easy, and if it were, everyone would be doing it and *Integrity* in our culture would not be an issue.

We may never get to the point where we have infallible *Integrity* according to these steps. But that does not mean we should refuse to exert the effort. Each of us needs to strive to run the race laid out in front of us in the best way possible. This is what is required for *Leaders of Character*.

When we fail—and we will at times—we must get up again and strive to do better next time. That too is our choice. Each time we fail to act like a person of *Integrity*, we have the opportunity to practice *Courage* and *Humility* to admit our failure. It also takes *Courage* to choose to do better the next time. That is the type of practice it will take for us all to build up our *Integrity* muscles. How many missed free throws precede the excellence that the best shooters of all time display at the free-throw line?

It takes hard work, sweat, and pain to become the person each of us was designed to be. We will miss the mark at times, but that does not mean we should quit practicing. We can't quit working on our character if we want to be persons of *Integrity* and *Leaders of Character*.

> *"The time is always right to do what is right."*
> — **Martin Luther King Jr.**

Exercising *Integrity*: Time to Break a Sweat

We all have to prepare for challenges to our *Integrity*. The good news is, our *Integrity* is tested daily. Every day we have choices that are the workouts that will prepare us for the heavy lifting on the horizon.

Our culture too often tells us, "Don't break a sweat. Having *Integrity* is not a big deal." But *Leaders of Character* are part of the counterculture! We must look at every opportunity to exercise *Integrity*, knowing that each test is a BIG DEAL! Without exercising our *Integrity* muscles, we will be unprepared when the even BIGGER DEAL emerges.

Leaders of Character have *Integrity* because they have the *Courage* to stand up for what is right, even when it comes with a personal cost. They go beyond knowing what to do in a tough situation. They exercise the *Courage* to take action and then explain why they acted. Because they have the *Courage* to do the right thing, they also understand the concepts of *Duty* and *Selflessness*. Each of these *Habits of Character* are interrelated.

Here is a list of exercises that any of us can accomplish. It does not matter whether you have been exercising *Integrity* for years, or you recently realized you are weak in this area. Each time you choose to exercise *Integrity* in the areas described below, you will find it easier to make that same choice again. That is how habits are formed, one choice at a time. With each new choice that builds your *Integrity*, you will get closer and closer to creating the *Habit of Character* we call *Integrity*.

Overall

- ✓ Tell the waitress she forgot to include on your bill the desert you ate .
- ✓ Tell the policeman the exact speed you were going when he asks, "Do you know how fast you were going?"
- ✓ Follow through with excellence on a commitment that you now wish you hadn't made.
- ✓ Do not wait until you are already late to contact the person you are supposed to meet.
- ✓ Have that tough conversation you have been putting off.
- ✓ Whether you say "yes" or "no", mean it without qualification.
- ✓ Check your motives before you confront someone to be sure you are not speaking up for selfish reasons.
- ✓ Confront an employee, a peer, a spouse, or a supervisor when you recognize a shortcoming in them.
- ✓ Say "no" instead of making a commitment you cannot keep and still do your best.

At Work

- ✓ When your supervisor asks for your opinion, give it truthfully, even if she may not like what you have to say.
- ✓ Accept responsibility for missing a deadline without making an excuse.
- ✓ When your supervisor asks, "What happened?" be the first to speak up and take responsibility.
- ✓ Drive back to work after 5 p.m. to fulfill a commitment to a co-worker you forgot about.

At Home

- ✓ Give the same level of determination to a commitment you made to your spouse or child as you do to the commitments you make to your boss.
- ✓ Apologize and ask for forgiveness from your children or spouse when you make a mistake.

✓ Don't back out on a commitment you made to your spouse or child without asking for forgiveness for breaking a promise to them.

✓ Make your child do her own work on all her school projects.

✓ Tell your spouse the whole story, even if it will upset him or her.

✓ Point out *Integrity* issues in the news to your family and make them a learning opportunity.

✓ Whenever possible, never be late paying a bill or slow repaying a loan.

Chapter 7

HABIT #4: SELFLESSNESS

The Warm-Up: Questions for Stretching Your Mind

Who is the most selfless person you know? _____

On a scale from 1 to 10, with 10 meaning saintly selflessness, where do you rate yourself when it comes to being selfless? _____

What rating would your friends _____, family, _____, and coworkers _____ give you?

The General's Story: *A Pilot Does More Than He Has to Do*

To understand the meaning of *Selflessness*, we must begin with the understanding that to be selfless ties into *Humility* and requires an approach to situations and relationships that says, "It is not about me."

On the battlefield, I witnessed many acts of *Selflessness*. One in particular occurred in late May 1970. I was a battalion commander, and our Area of Operation was in Cambodia. We were on the same offensive into Cambodia that included the retrieval of our soldiers' bodies from the bunker complex—a story I shared with you earlier. At this particular time, we were still operating out of Fire Support Base DAVID.

I sent our scout platoon on a reconnaissance mission to verify intelligence on an enemy cache site. The platoon got into a firefight with the enemy, and the scout platoon leader was seriously wounded. While in my command-and-control helicopter checking on our four rifle companies, the call came over the radio for a medevac helicopter to pick up the wounded lieutenant.

I heard the operations officer say, "The medevac has gone to refuel and will be at your location in about one hour."

"We cannot wait for an hour," the medic responded. "I am having difficulty stopping the bleeding, and he may be dead in an hour."

I got on the intercom to the pilot and asked him if we could land and pick up our wounded officer. This helicopter had top-secret electronics equipment and the pilots were responsible for the security of that equipment. So it was the pilot's call to take the risk, not mine. He had the option of saying, "Sir, we cannot afford to have the enemy capture this equipment. I am responsible for it."

Instead he simply said, "Sir, I am at your command. If you tell me that you want me to land this helicopter down there, I will do my best to put it where you need it to be."

At that point I called the operations officer and told him that we were in the area and we were coming in to pick up the wounded scout platoon leader.

The pilot put the helicopter down in the only place clear of trees. It was on the side of a steep hill where he could get only one skid on solid ground. I jumped out on the left side of the helicopter. When I hit the ground, I spotted a North Vietnamese soldier come out of the woods about fifty yards away. He was carrying a rocket propelled grenade launcher (RPG). He went to one knee, aiming the RPG at the helicopter as I pulled the trigger of my M16. Unfortunately, he fired the RPG right before the M16 rounds hit him. It looked like the missile was flying right at me. However, it passed just to my left, went under the tail boom of the helicopter, and exploded. I immediately lost my hearing, and for a period of three days my men had to write me messages if they had information I needed to know. A few small pieces of shrapnel punctured the tail boom. The pilot checked the chopper for any serious damages. Finding none, we loaded up the wounded officer, took off, and delivered him to the nearest aid station across the border in South Vietnam.

The gravely wounded platoon leader survived, thanks to the *Courage* and *Selflessness* of that pilot. He did not have to agree to land his chopper on the side of a hill under fire. He had every right to protect himself and the top-secret equipment he was responsible for. He performed a selfless act because he believed it was his *Duty* to help save that platoon leader, even at the cost of his own life. It may not have been his job to act as an evacuation chopper, but he recognized his moral obligation to try to help save the life of a fellow soldier.

Notice, he did not worry about the consequences if that vehicle he was responsible for had been destroyed or captured. He recognized that he was not bigger than the situation. He saw that the needs of another human being outweighed his own. His act of *Selflessness* took *Courage* and a sense of *Duty* that we should try to emulate as *Leaders of Character*.

The Business Guy's Story: *The Leader Takes One for the Team*

During my years in sales, we would often initiate dinners at nice restaurants with our clients. At every dinner, we brought in well-respected experts to provide the latest and most accurate information available. However, some individuals in the industry abused this process to the point where a string of government regulations were setup to monitor all these dinner programs. Our company, in an attempt to steer clear of any hint of wrongdoing, interpreted and enforced the rules beyond what the government required.

One particular situation that occurred under these rules is a great illustration of selfless leadership in business. One regulation the company established to ensure no perception of impropriety was to require a minimum number of attendees at each dinner. On one occasion, when two sales personnel failed to get enough people to attend one of the sponsored dinners, their sales manager received a call from his regional director. The sales manager had already done his homework and was satisfied that the two sales people had done everything they could to get people to attend the dinner. In fact, twenty-four hours before the dinner, the sales people had well over the required number of RSVPs.

On the day of the dinner, the sales people faxed reminder invitations, sent reminder text messages, and even called each of the confirmed RSVP's offices to reconfirm. But despite all the confirmations leading up to the dinner, only one guest showed. Though the regional director was a well-respected and levelheaded person, he insisted that the sales manager "write up" the sales people for the infraction of the regulation. His concern was for the perception government investigators might have if they looked into the low attendance.

His argument was definitely plausible and would cover himself, the manager, and the company should government authorities ever investigate the matter. But it would not help the sales people who would have a write-up in their file that could affect raises, promotions, or even employment. Though the sales manager argued vehemently—"They did everything possible to get people to the dinner, short of picking them up themselves"—the regional director refused to budge due to the highly regulated business environment.

That was when the sales manager took one for the team. He told the regional director, "Then *you* write *me* up for refusal to write-up my people as directed. That way, if anyone is held responsible for anything, it will be me and not two of our best people who did everything in their control to have a different outcome."

The regional director fell silent. Then he tried again to make his case. But the sales manager stuck to his guns and insisted that the regional director write-up him instead of his team members. In the end, the regional director backed down, and no one was charged with an infraction.

In today's highly regulated business environment, many people might think that the sales manager was foolish for making a stand the way he did. However, he placed the needs of those he led ahead of his own needs. That is what *Selflessness* looks like and does. When he stood up and held firm, he coupled moral *Courage* and *Selflessness* to ensure the right thing was done for two good sales people.

Defining *Selflessness*

From 2002 to 2007, the United States was a huge disappointment in basketball on the international level. America failed to medal in the 2002 World Championships, only earned a bronze medal in the 2004 Olympics, and settled for bronze again in the 2006 World Championships. But in 2008, the United States returned to dominance on the world basketball stage. The United States decisively won the gold medal at the Olympics in Beijing and has not failed to win gold in any international competitions since. What made the difference? A coach who preached *Selflessness*.

The change in the US Olympic team's fortunes is detailed in the book *The Gold Standard*, written by Coach Mike Krzyzewski. In 2008, Coach K was working with the most talented players in the world, just as previous teams' coaches had. He had players who professionally made millions of dollars and yet played for free for their country, just as they had done for other coaches in previous international competitions. The 2008 team had players who were considered the "go to guy" on each of their NBA teams, just as the previous teams had. So what did Coach K get his Olympic team to do that other coaches had failed to do? He got his players to behave selflessly. The difference between the teams of the early 2000s and the teams since 2008 is *Selflessness*. Egos and one-upmanship were set aside. Players played for each other, for the team, for their coach, for their country. Self was swallowed up into something greater.

Unlike the international media attention these Olympic wins received, selfless acts by regular people are rarely highlighted on the news. Maybe one reason for this is that *Selflessness* and *Humility* are intertwined. Selfless people don't boast about their unselfish actions. They are humble people.

A great example of *Humility* preceding *Selflessness* comes from the 1970s movie *Brian's Song*. While the movie focused on the football careers of Gale Sayers and his best friend Brian Piccalo, it was more about selfless service and friendship. The movie was based on the book *I Am Third*, by Gale Sayers. Sayers' mantra in his book is:

God is first.
Others are second.
And I am third.

Selfless people, because they do not need the spotlight, do not bring attention to themselves. They put others first. They take seriously Rick Warren's motto from his book *The Purpose-Driven Life*: "It's not about me." They live out this approach to life in what they say and do. In other words, *Humility*—believing and acting like "It is not about me"—and *Selflessness* are inseparable *Habits of Character*. Because of *Humility*, a *Leader of Character* is able to act selflessly.

Andersons' 12-Word (or less) Definition of Selflessness
Putting the needs of others before my own needs, desires, or convenience

---

Common synonyms for *Selflessness*:
benevolence, kindness, charity, magnanimity

Courage and *Selflessness* are intertwined when we have to sacrifice something we need or desire in order to put others first. The courageous acts of the pilot in *The General's* story are vivid examples of *Selflessness* and *Courage* working together in the same person.

Integrity and *Selflessness* depend on each other as well because motives matter when it comes to *Integrity*. *Selflessness* is often the motivation that will drive leaders to step forward and take responsibility for the missteps of their team members, as in *The Business Guy's* story.

It is *Selflessness* that makes a heroic act possible. Heroic acts are not what we do to save ourselves. An act is heroic when we put ourselves at risk for others. Furthermore, just because someone acts with *Courage* or does the right thing does not necessarily make her a hero or a *Leader of Character*. Motives matter too. If the reasons for her actions stem from self-preservation or self-promotion, then we should think twice about labeling her act heroic or saying that her behavior displayed high character. Making the choice to act is one thing, but making that choice for the right reasons is another.

At the same time, selfless *Leaders of Character* do not fall for the lies that tell leaders they are entitled because they have an important title. They never get the entitlement attitude because they are thankful for the opportunity to lead others. Selfless leaders do not feel entitled; they feel responsible. They see the role of leader as a calling to serve, not to be served. Therefore they demand more from themselves than they do from others.

> Selfless leaders do not feel entitled; they feel responsible. They see the role of leader as a calling to serve, not to be served. Therefore they demand more from themselves than they do from others.

The *Selflessness* that *Leaders of Character* display comes from the attitude they have about their role on the team or in the family. If a leader is not devoted to developing the individuals on his team, then that leader is not leading. Rather, that person is probably managing. The *Leader of Character* believes that you *lead* people and you *manage* resources. People are not just tools a leader uses to get things done. People are the primary responsibility of a *Leader of Character,* and therefore their growth is his top priority. After all, if other people are not growing as a result of our leadership, then we must be focused on the wrong things.

The Choice: Selfishness or *Selflessness*

Selfishness is an epidemic in the workplace, in our children, and in our homes. The idea that looking out for #1 is an admirable trait or that it is the only way to succeed in today's culture is a lie.

In the business world, too many leaders believe that the people they lead are there to serve them when, in fact, the exact opposite is the case. Maybe it is the ignorance that inexperience brings, maybe it is a character issue that has been there since they were young, but some leaders take over leadership positions and believe that the people they lead owe them something. They believe the team they lead should follow them without hesitation, that loyalty is deserved and trust should be unquestioned. They believe that because they have the title of leader, everyone else is there to do their bidding. The positional authority these people wield may work for a time, but what the selfish leader gets is compliance, not commitment.

When the leader looks out for #1, the team develops the same mentality. Selfishness and the desire for recognition take over. An "every man for himself" attitude causes a group of talented players to perform well below their capabilities.

Just like in the Olympics, the competency (talent) of the players means little if they do not have the character (*Selflessness*) to play together.

A selfish leader is the death knell for any organization, team, or family. You can spot them, no matter the setting or stress level. Whatever the situation, we have a choice to make between selfishness and *Selflessness*.

Selfishness Versus *Selflessness*

Selfishness: Choosing to ask sales people to load accounts at the end of the year so the leader can win an award.
Selflessness: Choosing to miss out on personal awards or recognition so the individuals on your team are not behind on their sales numbers to begin the following year.

Selfishness: Choosing to use phrases like "*My* team," "He works for *me*," and "This is how *I* did it."
Selflessness: Choosing to use phrases like "Our team," "We work together," and "This is what the team accomplished."

Selfishness: Choosing to be consistently late to the meetings you called.
Selflessness: Choosing to be consistently on time to meetings with your people, as if you had to be on time for the CEO.

Selfishness: Choosing to say "I'm here for you" to the individuals who work for you, but rarely making time for more than a passing comment or a surface conversation.
Selflessness: Choosing to give individuals your undivided attention and listening to them.

Selfishness: Choosing not to promote qualified people off the team because you might lose a valued employee.

Selflessness: Choosing to do everything in your power to help others reach their goals.

Selfishness: Choosing not to listen to others and instead just waiting to talk.
Selflessness: Choosing to listen carefully to others before formulating your opinions or offering a response.

Selfishness: Choosing to hold back resources from the team so you can come in under budget.
Selflessness: Choosing to provide every available resource in order to give everyone the best chance to succeed.

Because a *Leader of Character* is both humble and selfless, she realizes that relationship building is a critical part of leadership. The managerial and administrative demands that come with the title of leader may be overwhelming, but she knows success is merely a dream without her team. To get the buy-in of her team, she needs to build relationships with them.

As we discussed, leadership is about people. We cannot and should not consider ourselves *Leaders of Character* if we do not work on building relationships with the people around us.

But what if you are not relationally oriented? What if your personality type shows that you are more task-oriented? What if you are instinctually an introvert? Well then, you need to understand that our personalities are not our destinies. We should not use our personalities as an excuse for not growing. Just because you (and the rest of us) have a natural tendency to behave in one manner does not mean you cannot choose to behave in another. Choosing a new behavior that is contrary to our instincts will make us uncomfortable. That's normal, even expected. Yet, if we choose to only do the things that make us comfortable, then we are putting our comfort in front of the needs of the people we lead. If we do that, our leadership is really about us, not about those who follow us.

Of course, it also possible for those of us who are naturally outgoing and relationally oriented to fall into a habit of developing relationships only for our own good. We can build relationships and use them for our own advancement. We can be relationally selfish! So even in our many relationships, we need to engage with unselfish motives. *Leaders of Character* enter into every interaction with another person with the object of making the other person better. It does not matter whether the other person works for that leader or is an attendant at the convenience store. *Leaders of Character* see every interaction as an opportunity to develop a relationship focused on the other person.

So ask yourself, "I may never see that convenience store attendant again, but how did I leave him after that interaction? Did I leave him better, or did I leave him worse?" Remember, you have influence over everyone you interact with. Whether you are in a work setting or in a restaurant at lunchtime, you have the opportunity to influence someone's life positively or negatively. So keep this question in mind with each person you meet and engage: "Is that person in a better place now after being with me?" If the answer is yes, then you are likely acting selflessly.

Everything you do and say can have either a positive affect or a negative affect on others. If your children are watching you (and they are always watching), then you are influencing the next generation of leaders. The same goes with you at work, playing on a sports team, coaching, leading at your place of worship, and so on. You are on public display, and you have influence on people everyday. It is up to you to decide if you are going to leave the people you meet in a better place or a worse one than they were before you interacted with them.

Please don't think that because you lack a title like vice president or supervisor that you do not have an opportunity to lead where you are. An essential aspect of leadership is influence. All of us exercise influence, for good or for bad. And those who are *Leaders of Character* use their influence for the good of others. You can use the influence you have to lead others in ways that will benefit them. Or, if you choose to lead out of self-interest, you will be an ineffective leader and probably a lousy spouse, parent, friend, child, and co-worker.

Choosing to act selflessly doesn't take a lot of time or effort either. For instance, you can take a second to thank the man cleaning the restrooms in your office building or take the little bit of time and effort needed to ask your waitress her name at lunch. Those simple daily choices can positively influence those people and add value to them. If, on the other hand, you choose to do nothing and walk past such individuals as if they were nothing more than a piece of furniture, your actions can negatively influence them. The choice is yours. You *will* exercise influence. The only real option you have is to use your influence selfishly or selflessly.

> *Selflessness does not require me to think*
> *less of myself but to think of myself less.*

One way God has separated man from beast is by giving us the ability to move beyond our instincts. We can make other choices. And each time we make a choice, it makes it easier to make that choice again in the future. That is how habits are formed. And among the many choices we can make is the choice between selfishness and *Selflessness*. We can choose to live to self or to others. We don't have to live with self-preservation, self-advancement, and self-involvement as our dominant mode of behavior. We can do much better than that. And that is a choice *Leaders of Character* consistently make.

Selflessness and *Leaders of Character*

Selflessness is so rare in today's culture that a truly selfless person sticks out in the crowd. While some leaders are focused on how they look, getting their way, or maintaining their own comfort or convenience, the *Leader of Character* does the opposite. You can recognize a *Leader of Character* because everything she does says "I'm in it for you!" Her leadership is not characterized by "my way or the highway" kind of thinking. She truly wants the best way. *Leaders of Character* will sacrifice their own comfort or convenience for someone else whether that person can help them or not. They display *Selflessness* because their first goal is to make other people better.

> You can recognize a *Leader of Character* because
> everything she does says "I'm in it for you!"

Let's consider the various traits of selfless leaders.

Selfless People Add Value to Others

Even the best team strategies or the most beneficial feedback will be filtered through perceived motives. If those perceptions are negative, then the leader will not be credible. For leaders this includes those hard conversations that go with coaching performance. When those conversations begin, leaders need to think, *Does the individual I'm coaching believe I am here for me, for the company, or for him?* If he believes we are there for ourselves, then our impact on him will be minimal and fleeting. This is the same in families as well. If a child believes the parent is more worried about appearances or the family reputation than the child herself, then the parent's efforts will likely be for naught.

Likewise, sometimes leaders coach people and the message sent is, "You must get better so the company hits its numbers." The message here is, "You are just a tool we use to increase our profits." What the employee hears is, "I need you to do this so we can get more production out of you." With motives like that, are we surprised when a leader has unengaged team members?

With the selfless leader, there is rarely a question of motive. Since she has proven through her behaviors that she is not in it for herself and that she truly cares about us as individuals, we view her motives as genuine and her credibility with us increases.

In his book *The 21 Irrefutable Laws of Leadership,* John Maxwell states that the role of the leader is to "Add value to others." Selfless people make the best coaches because they are truly dedicated to making people better by adding value to them. Their *Humility* drives them to put the growth of others first and to believe and act like "It's not about me."

This goes along with the principles of servant leadership that multiple authors have detailed. One of the best books on the topic of servant leadership was written by Dave's friend, Jim Hunter, and titled *The Servant*. *Selflessness* is the foundation to becoming a servant leader, just as it is essential to becoming a *Leader of Character*. Jim Hunter points out that the servant leader is not in it for herself. She is there to serve those she leads rather than having them serve her. She is 100 percent dedicated to doing what is best for the people she leads. Now, this does not make her a pushover. On the contrary, the servant leader is as adept at administering discipline as in giving out hugs.

Selfless people are great leaders because they put the needs of the team and the individuals on the team before their own needs or desires. This also applies to tough talks. Selfless leaders will have uncomfortable conversations with employees because it is in the employees' best interest. Selfless leaders will take the time to coach and develop the people on their team. The leader is committed to the success of the led. Selfless leaders are not there to be served but to serve. They have the *Humility* to do that. *Leaders of Character* do not see employees as tools for their own success. These leaders believe that their role is to help others become the best version of themselves as they can be.

One way to become that selfless *Leader of Character* and focus on developing others is to develop a mentor's attitude. We can develop that attitude by consistently asking ourselves this simple question:

"Is that person in a better place now after being with me?"

For instance, great coaches are great because they see every interaction as an opportunity to help another person grow. *Leaders of Character* are not consumed with the other requirements of leading. Instead they are consumed with the idea that they have a *Duty* to help make each person a better version of himself. Because they serve the needs of others first, other people grow and they willingly follow them.

Selfless People Are the Best Teammates

The best teammates are selfless. They are the ones who put individual goals, accolades, or convenience behind what is best for the team and their teammates. The 2015 NBA champions, the Golden State Warriors, had perhaps the best player in the league that season in Stephan Curry. But the man who won the finals MVP award was Andre Igboudala. Igboudala had started every single game of his eleven-year NBA career, but when his coach asked him to begin coming off the bench for the 2015 season, he accepted his new role as a substitute. Because of this he played fewer minutes and averaged less than eight points per game in 2015, but he still helped his team to the best record in the NBA. He understood his role on that team and put his own individual statistics and goals behind the needs of his team.

He was rewarded in the NBA finals when his coach, Steve Kerr, decided he needed new energy on the court to overcome LeBron James and the Cleveland Cavaliers. Igboudala was the spark plug that led the Warriors to victory, earning him the MVP award. That would have never been possible if he had not put his team first.

Selfless people make the best teammates because they do not need the spotlight all the time. They see themselves as no more important than anyone else, even if they are the best player on the field or the court. Selfless teammates willingly offer to help others. They spend time ensuring their teammates get credit for their contributions. They are more concerned about the final outcome than with how they look while achieving that outcome.

Selfless teammates lend a helping hand to another person, even when it is inconvenient for them. All of us have days when we feel like we don't want to do something, such as helping another person. That is especially the case when offering that help could cause us to fall behind, be late, or repeat work we have already done ourselves. But selfless teammates help out, no matter the cost to them.

Selfless teammates can be counted on to do the hard things. They will step up and volunteer. They will take responsibility when others hesitate. They make these choices because they do not believe that their own needs or convenience come before what is good for the team.

Selfless teammates can be counted on to do the hard things. They will step up and volunteer. They will take responsibility when others hesitate.

Selfless People Listen to Others

We all know "that guy" we want to run from at cocktail parties. The one who dominates every conversation. The one who talks about himself, his accomplishments, his week, his children, his work, his boss, his whatever. The one who always seems to have a story to top yours. When you break it all down, what does "that guy" sound like? "Me, Me, Me, Me, Me … oh, and did I mention Me?"

On the opposite end of the spectrum is the person who, when you are done speaking with her, you feel like the most important person in the world. You feel so good about yourself that you want to be around her more. You may know someone like that. How do you feel after you are with her? Do you feel like she cares about you? Do you feel like she cares about your opinions? Whether a man or a woman, people who listen well show how much they care. They understand something about other people …

They don't care how much you know until they know how much you care.

Listening is one of the best ways to let people know you care about them. That is why selfish people are such bad listeners. The selfish person's need to be the center of the conversation lets everyone around him know that he thinks he's the most important person in the room. Therefore, selfish people have very few real friends or followers, because no one is under any delusion that they truly care one iota about anyone but themselves. If a leader is not a good listener, then he probably has few real followers.

Because selfless people put themselves behind others, they make the other person the most important person in a conversation. They ask questions and they wait for the answers. They live by God's math: God gave us two ears and one mouth, so we need to use them proportionately.

> They live by God's math: God gave us two ears and
> one mouth, so we need to use them proportionately.

Our good friend Steve Wiley of the Lincoln Leadership Institute is fond of saying, "Listen until it hurts." It takes effort and concentration to give someone your undivided attention. It is even harder for those of us who fight selfishness in our character. Our willingness to listen until it hurts is a direct reflection on how we view our own importance. When we are so enamored with the sound of our own voice that we never really hear what the other person is saying, we are providing a window into our character. When we are struggling to listen, we are probably struggling with pride and selfishness.

To listen until it hurts takes a level of *Humility* and *Selflessness* that can only be acquired through practice. To be a *Leader of Character*, we must DO what we want to BE. If we want to be selfless, we must begin to practice listening better and acting selflessly in our conversations.

In some conversations we may find ourselves nodding knowingly while strategizing our rebuttal. That is not listening. Being a good listener requires that we break this habit.

Dr. Henry Cloud in his book *Integrity* states, "True listening and understanding has not occurred until the other person understands that you understand." One of the most effective techniques for doing this is called "Active Listening." Active listening involves repeating back to the other person what you think he just said. "What I am hearing from you is …. Is that correct?" This is an amazingly simple practice, and you will be astounded how many misunderstandings are avoided when you use Active Listening.

Whether we decide to listen twice as much as we talk, "listen until it hurts," or utilize Active Listening, our willingness to become better listeners is a direct reflection on our character. When the people around us know they are truly being heard, they will also believe that their leader is a humble and selfless *Leader of Character*.

Selfless People Have Great Attitudes

Have you ever met anyone who had a bad attitude and yet was truly a selfless person, someone who routinely served others? The habit of *Positivity* gets a whole chapter in this book where we dig into this topic, including the causes of a bad attitude. Suffice it to say here that selfless people rarely, if ever, exhibit a bad attitude. When you look at the most selfless persons you know, how often do you see them in a bad mood? How frequently do you see selfless people complaining or dragging down the mood in a room? Selfless people almost always have great attitudes about their circumstances and life in general.

Does *Selflessness* create positive attitudes, or do positive attitudes create *Selflessness*? Does the answer to that question even matter? The key is, if we begin to focus our behaviors on serving others in selfless ways, our attitude will follow and become more positive. That is why so many people who go on short-term missions trips come back with a different attitude about life. They have served and served unselfishly.

Like everything else about character and leadership we have discussed so far, our attitude is a choice. We have the ability to choose our attitude everyday. If we choose each day to exhibit *Positivity*, we will probably also choose to act selflessly as well. *Positivity* and *Selflessness* go hand in hand.

Selfless Leaders Are Credible, Build Trust, and Gain Commitment

Selflessness leads to credibility. Credibility fosters trust. Trust brings commitment.

A leader without the credibility and trust that begins with *Selflessness* will find himself in the role of micromanager. He will be pulling every carrot-and-stick motivational tool from the managerial toolbox in order to keep his team moving. That leader will be worn out and wondering why his team is not as committed to excellence as he is. When the fact is, the members of his team are not committed to him, and they are only submitting to him.

When someone cares more about others than he does himself, we pay more attention when he speaks. If you know someone who has a reputation for looking out for himself first, are you likely to follow him or even listen to him? On the other hand, when someone behaves selflessly, we tend to listen to him intently. We know that what he is doing or wants to do comes from unselfish motives.

If a leader's motives are disingenuous or even unclear, his credibility suffers. Credibility is an important component to trust. If we are credible, our motives will be trusted. "Dave does what is right for me. He has always put others before himself. I trust what he is saying or doing." Without that trust, what a leader gets is short-term compliance and not long-term commitment. When people know the leader is motivated to see them grow, they will accept criticism and tough conversations. They will trust the leader's motives are selfless, and therefore they will go beyond compliance and willingly and enthusiastically follow, even if the conversation stung. When a leader's behaviors demonstrate a desire to see the individual grow and get better, the leader can say some hard things to someone and still see an increase in commitment from the one coached. "Ow. That hurt. But I know he is in it for me and just trying to make me better."

Trust between the leader and the led brings commitment. A leader who builds credibility through selfless actions and attitudes has the credibility that creates the trust necessary for people to commit to even the most difficult strategies.

Exercising *Selflessness*: Time to Break a Sweat

Just like any of the other *Habits of Character* we have discussed, if we do not act selflessly in the day-to-day decisions of our lives, we are unlikely to act unselfishly in the big moments. *Selflessness* is a habit that is developed through practice. The day-to-day practice of selfless acts will develop a *Habit of Character* that will prepare us for the big challenges in our future. Here are some drills we can all do in practice so when it's game time, *Selflessness* will be an ingrained *Habit of Character*.

Overall
- ✓ Maintain eye contact with people, even when your phone buzzes.
- ✓ Leave everybody in a better condition than when you found them.
- ✓ Clear other people's dishes from the table without being asked.

✓ Anonymously pay for someone else's meal, gas, or tolls.

✓ Never tip less than 20 percent no matter the service you received.

✓ When it is raining, share your umbrella with a stranger or give it to them.

✓ Look everyone in the eye and greet them no matter their title.

✓ Find out some personal information about a person who is serving you (be that person a waiter, driver, cashier, etc.).

✓ Use Active Listening: repeat back what you think you heard the other person (your spouse, child, friends, co-workers) said before you respond.

✓ Pull over and help a stranger change a tire and tell no one about what you did.

At Work

✓ Set individual goals with a team member and do everything in your power to help him or her achieve those goals.

✓ Strive to be the last person to speak in a meeting instead of the first.

✓ Regularly get your assistant a cup of coffee.

✓ Ask more questions and make fewer statements.

✓ Close your computer when someone walks into your office to talk to you or calls you.

✓ Deflect praise from yourself and give credit to someone else.

✓ Stay late at work to help a peer or a subordinate complete a project.

✓ Take the time to write a thank-you note to someone who is not in a position to benefit you.

✓ End every conversation by asking, "What do you need from me? How can I help you today?"

At Home

✓ Fulfill a promise to your child, even if it means it will make work more difficult for you later.

✓ Serve your spouse every day without expecting anything in return.

✓ Turn off or pause the TV when a family member is speaking with you.

✓ Drop whatever you are doing when you are asked for help by your spouse or child.

✓ Make your spouse's favorite dinner.

✓ Go on a "date night," even if you had a long day.

✓ Don't keep score in any relationship.

Chapter 8

HABIT #5: DUTY

The Warm-Up: Questions for Stretching Your Mind

Who is the person you can always count on to fulfill their obligations no matter what? _____

On a scale of 1 to 10, with 1 as the lowest and 10 as the highest, where do you rate yourself on fulfilling your obligations? _____

When was the last time you failed to fulfill an obligation? _____

The General's Story: *The Cooks' Counterattack*

On the battlefield, every soldier has the moral obligation to protect other soldiers. All good soldiers see this as part of their *Duty*. I saw soldiers who demonstrated this even when engaging the enemy was not one of their primary duties. One such incident occurred in Cambodia in late May 1970 at Fire Support Base (FSB) DAVID. This FSB was built to provide a base of operation for the battalion. It was built with a star-shaped pattern. But instead of the typical five points, the pattern had twenty points with sixty bunkers that had overhead protection. Each bunker had three or four infantry soldiers defending it. The FSB was about 150 meters long by 60 meters wide. We also had three 105mm howitzers inside the base. The base was surrounded by triple concertina wire and about ten to fifteen claymore mines in front of each bunker. The Tactical Operation Center was also in the center of the FSB. The support soldiers—namely, the cooks, mechanics, signal operators, and the like—also had sleeping facilities within the central part of the FSB.

One night a large enemy force attacked the FSB and successfully penetrated the base by capturing three or four of the bunkers. Since all of the rifle company defending the base was within the sixty bunkers, the only reserve we had to use as a counterattacking force was what we called the "cooks, bakers, and candlestick makers" platoon. When we realized that several bunkers had been captured, I ordered the reserve to retake those bunkers. Now, you need to realize that these soldiers were not trained to engage the enemy. Nevertheless, a communications officer led them, and every one of them participated in the assault. They managed to recapture the bunkers and helped to reestablish the security of the FSB. These soldiers, individually and collectively, saw it as their moral obligation, their *Duty*, to help protect all the soldiers and equipment on the FSB. And they performed their *Duty* well and with *Courage*.

The Businessman's Story: *Saying "I Forgot"*

As the phone rang, I recognized my boss's telephone number on caller ID. I didn't think much of it at first. I had worked for him about eight months, and we had a good relationship. Both of us had been in our respective positions for a while but had recently been reorganized into the same region. Though I had only recently begun reporting to him, we quickly developed a mutual respect for each other.

After some small talk on the phone, he got to the point. "I am calling because I was wondering when you were going to get that report to me."

My heart sank. I had no idea what he was talking about. "What report?"

"The one I was supposed to have from you yesterday by 5:00 p.m. I need to turn in the status for the entire region by noon today."

I took a long breath and said, "I am sorry, Dan. I forgot." There was a long awkward silence. I waited an uncomfortable period of time and then said, "Dan, are you there?"

"Yeah, I'm still here, Dave."

"Are you okay, Dan?"

"Yeah. I am just processing what you said. I have been doing this job for twelve years, and this is the first time any of my leaders ever just admitted they forgot." There was more silence and then he asked, "When can you get it to me?"

"It will be in your email in the next forty-five minutes."

He paused again, said thanks in a still confused manner, and hung up.

I was stunned. I couldn't believe that over a twelve-year period that not a single one of Dan's leaders had ever simply forgot to send him something. I forget things everyday. I am not proud of that, but I do not think I am alone in this. I knew the leaders who reported to Dan did not have perfect memories; they forgot things too. But I quickly concluded they never confessed forgetfulness. Instead they had a bad habit that most of us have—the habit of making excuses.

Duties are not performed for duty's sake, but because their neglect would make the man uncomfortable.

– Mark Twain

Defining *Duty*

Ask a veteran why he or she served and you will likely hear the word *Duty* in the explanation. The concept of *Duty* still runs deep in military circles.

Many people use the word *duty* to describe the list of tasks in a job description. But the idea of *Duty* goes well beyond a "to-do list." *Duty* seems to be a forgotten principle outside the military. The concept of *Duty* needs a revival.

The military may be one of the last places where the term *duty* is used and understood by the majority. In fact, West Point's motto puts *Duty* right up front.

West Point Motto: Duty – Honor – Country

West Point's motto is made up of three words with *Duty* heading the list.

Duty is doing what needs to be done without waiting for direction. *Duty* is seeing the need and doing it yourself. *Duty* is not worrying about whose job it is. *Duty* means that I see a need, and I take care of the need because it is what I should do.

In the business world, what the military calls *Duty* is often called accountability. Unfortunately, the term *accountability* is often misinterpreted as something you do to other people. You hold others accountable for their actions, or others hold you accountable for your actions. But this leaves off something extremely important. Should we not also hold ourselves accountable for our own actions? This is something we tend to avoid. In fact, most of us even recoil from the prospect of putting ourselves in a place where we are accountable to other people. We are much more willing, in our sinful, selfish perspective, to see the problems others have before we hold ourselves to those same standards. We will point out the stick in someone's eye and ignore the log in our own. That is why we asked you at the start of this chapter to think about your own record of fulfilling obligations to others.

Andersons' 12-Word (or less) Definition of Duty
Taking action based on our assigned tasks and moral obligations

---

Common synonyms for *Duty*: responsibility,
obligation, task, assignment, calling, job

Let's consider some essential characteristics of *Duty*.

Assigned Tasks

No matter where we are in life, there are certain tasks we are assigned to do. As kids we were assigned homework. As adults we now have job descriptions that spell out our assigned tasks. We also have leaders who may assign us tasks that are outside of our formal job descriptions.

As long as we have committed to a position or a role in an organization or a family and we are not asked to do something illegal or immoral, each of us has an obligation to complete those tasks. Accomplishing the tasks assigned to us by people in authority is also part of our *Duty*.

For a *Leader of Character,* assigned tasks become moral obligations as soon as we commit to them or agree to get paid for doing them. When we are hired to do a job, it is our moral obligation to accomplish our assigned tasks to the best of our abilities. The *Leader of Character* sees assigned tasks as moral obligations. That is where *Competence* (assigned tasks) and *Character* (moral obligations) overlap, and *Integrity* and *Duty* intersect.

Moral Obligations

We all have moral obligations in life. Senior leadership, middle management, and frontline workers should all understand they have certain moral obligations. We may have a different list of tasks in our job descriptions, such as developing strategies, managing finances, or organizing work teams, but we all have moral obligations within those positions.

Husbands and wives, and fathers and mothers also have tasks we assume responsibility for at home, whether it be cleaning, cooking, or paying the bills. But we also have moral obligations within the family. Just like in the workplace, these obligations may not be spelled out by law or even specifically voiced by another person, but they are still moral obligations.

Wherever we are serving or leading, fulfilling our moral obligations requires *Integrity and Courage*. We must have the *Integrity* to understand that we committed to doing more than just a list of assigned tasks, and we should exercise the *Courage* to take action based on that understanding.

As we stated in the chapter on *Integrity*, we can be an unethical rule followers. We have a moral obligation to go beyond just following the rules. If there is no rule against something, that does not make it okay to do. We must use our *Integrity*, fall back on what we know to be right, good, and proper, and then act on it. That is our moral obligation as a *Leader of Character*. That is our *Duty*.

Duty Is Not Feeling Dependent

Following through on my moral obligations should not be dependent on how I feel about them. Neither should following through be dependent on how I feel at that particular moment. What I should do is different from how I feel about what I should do. Emotions matter, but they should not dictate what I ought to do. The ethical right supersedes the emotional pull. When I accepted my role as the leader of the team or of my family, I gave up the right to only do what I feel like doing. It does not matter if I am having a bad day. It does not matter if I am unmotivated by the task. It does not matter if it is easy or hard for me based on my personality. My feelings as a leader are irrelevant when it comes to doing my *Duty*. As a *Leader of Character,* I must recognize I have to act on my moral obligations no matter how I feel about them.

> When I accepted my role as the leader of the team or of my family, I gave up the right to only do what I feel like doing.

On a team, whether it is an infantry platoon, a project team, a night shift, or a family, as long as they understand the concept of *Duty,* they know that it is unacceptable for things to be left undone or half done. And if that ever happens, everyone on the team knows it was their responsibility to fulfill the task no matter if it was in their individual job description. The team holds each other accountable for getting things done, and each member on the team holds himself accountable too. The leader is not the dispenser of all accountability because the individuals understand what *Duty* means. When a person understands *Duty* and consistently makes the choice to do their *Duty* instead of being unreliable, that person is forming an essential *Habit of Character.*

Too many people believe that as long as they complete the tasks required or specifically described by their boss, their spouse, or some law, that they are doing enough.

Perhaps that is why we have so many people who only do the minimum required.

Perhaps that is why we have so many companies that never go beyond mediocrity.

Perhaps that is why we have so many marriages that are at the brink of failure.

Perhaps that is why we have a society that is self-absorbed and largely ignores the plight of the less fortunate.

Perhaps that is why we need to reinvigorate the concept of *Duty* in our own lives and the lives of the people we have influence over. We need to remind people what *Duty* is and how it works.

Being *Duty* Bound

> *"There is nothing in the universe that I fear, but that I shall not know all my duty, or shall fail to do it."*
>
> **– Mary Lyon**

If I am a *Leader of Character*, *Duty* is not just a concept. *Duty* is an essential *Habit of Character* that guides who I am and how I make decisions. I am literally "*Duty* bound." I am tied to my moral obligations and cannot get away from them.

The people who are *Duty* bound often see the big picture. They know they are a part of something much bigger than themselves. But they also believe they are critical to the mission. Because they are selfless and see the big picture, they see the ripple effects of their own failure to act. They know that if they do not take action—do their *Duty*—it will affect everyone around them. They truly understand that their actions do not take place in a vacuum. For every action there is a reaction. If they do not do what they should do, then someone else will have to do it.

There is a sense of shame that wells up inside of a *Duty*-bound person when she fails to perform her *Duty*. Not only has she let her team down, but she has let herself down. She has allowed a distorted sense of *Duty* to take over. She took the cheap and easy way out. She did not choose the harder and better right. She was weak and chose the easier wrong.

We need to revive a sense of *Duty*. To do that in our sphere of influence, we must be *Duty* bound ourselves. Only then can we influence our family and the people we work with towards the same level of moral obligation that drives us to do our *Duty*.

Remember, too, that *Duty* is what drives many of our heroes who have served our country. As they often say in response to praise, "I was just doing my *Duty*." And they mean that.

The Choice: Unreliability or *Duty*

Ask yourself, "If I do not complete my assigned tasks or my moral obligations, then who can count on me?" There may be a lot of ways to sugarcoat being unreliable, but as you may have gathered by now, we don't spend a lot of time sugarcoating things in this book. If you choose to do your *Duty*, then other people will know they are dealing with someone who can be trusted. As soon as you demonstrate a reluctance to do your *Duty*—taking action based on your assigned tasks and moral obligations—other people will always question your reliability and lose trust in you. And because of your choices, they will have every right to do so.

When it comes to *Duty*, all of us are judged by our choices. Whether we are in the habit of doing our *Duty* or being unreliable comes down to the consistent choices we make.

Unreliability Versus *Duty*

Unreliability: Choosing to skip a committee meeting at a non-profit you promised to serve on because it has been a long day.
Duty: Choosing to follow through on the commitment to the best of your ability no matter how you feel that day.

Unreliability: Choosing to procrastinate calling back a subordinate.
Duty: Choosing never to let a message go unacknowledged, even if you do not have the answer or the time to answer.

Unreliability: Choosing to limit yourself to your job description or the specifically declared standards of your supervisor.

Duty: Choosing to do your best work in every circumstance and do a task that needs to be done, even if it is not your specified task to do.

Unreliability: Choosing to promise to talk to your supervisor on behalf of an employee and never doing it.

Duty: Choosing to treat the promise to the employee as if it was a promise to your boss by following through and following up.

Unreliability: Choosing to blame circumstances or other people to explain away why you did not fulfill a commitment or do it with excellence.

Duty: Choosing to claim responsibility, to ask for forgiveness, and to work tirelessly to correct the situation.

Unreliability: Choosing not to take your child to the playground or to a ball game because you had a long day.

Duty: Choosing to fulfill every promise you make to your child no matter your current energy level.

Every time we choose to do our *Duty* instead of being unreliable, we have just won a test of our character.

We are choosing *Courage* and *Duty* when we fire a high-performing team member who is selfish and demeans others on the team. We have the *Courage* to do more than just generate business for our company because our *Duty* is also to the people we lead to create the best work environment possible for them.

We are choosing *Humility* and *Duty* when we choose to take our shopping cart back to the rack at the grocery store instead of leaving it in the parking lot because we believe it is our *Duty* to not add to the work of other people when it is in our power to do so.

We are choosing *Selflessness* and *Duty* when we leave the house late in order to help our spouse get two upset children ready for school because we believe it is our *Duty* to serve our spouse and family even when it is inconvenient.

When faced with choosing *Duty* or being unreliable, our *Courage*, our *Humility*, our *Integrity*, our *Selflessness*, and our *Positivity* are part of the test.

Duty and *Leaders of Character*

Duty and Effort

Too many people see standards as the level they need to aspire to reach. But standards are the minimum, not the ultimate goal. Unfortunately, some people believe life is about meeting the minimum expectations of others.

That's not the case for a *Leader of Character*. To such leaders, their *Duty* is to give their maximum effort to every endeavor. Their *Duty* is not to do some parts of their job well. Rather, their *Duty* is to consistently give every part of their job everything they have. If we only do the stuff we like to do or work only to achieve the minimum standards, our effort is a reflection of our character. When we commit to do anything, whether it is a paid job or a volunteer role, *Leaders of Character* have a moral obligation to give maximum effort. Why? Because we gave our word when we committed to it. We signed on to do the task, whatever it may be and for whomever it may be. We chose to do the job—not in part, but in whole. We chose to give ourselves to it, not partially but fully. This is where *Duty* and *Integrity* overlap and become moral obligations.

Duty and Making Excuses

> *"You can't escape the responsibility of tomorrow by evading it today."*
> – **Abraham Lincoln**

But what if circumstances change? What if something happens, and we can't fulfill the commitments we made? Are we off the hook? Or are we still responsible for fulfilling those commitments?

We live in a world where people try to escape responsibility, especially blaming others for their mistakes. Lawyers make millions because individuals or billion dollar companies believe they have an excuse that justifies their actions. A *Leader of Character*, however, is countercultural. Unlike so many people in her culture, she does not make excuses. A *Leader of Character* takes responsibility, no matter the circumstances.

You see, we humans sometimes fail. We make mistakes. Our follow-through isn't always what it should be. And while there may be reasons for any particular failure, *Leaders of Character* do not excuse the breakdown. There is a difference between an excuse and a reason. An excuse is used to deflect responsibility, while a reason is something a *Leader of Character* takes responsibility for learning from in the future.

The *Leaders of Character* that West Point develops truly believe that there is no legitimate excuse when leaders fail. At West Point, a plebe's (freshman's) four acceptable responses are:

- Yes, sir.
- No, sir.
- No excuse, sir.
- Sir, I do not understand.

"No excuse, sir." Of the four approved responses, this one was hardest for most of us to say. "No excuse, sir" was designed to break our old habit of making excuses and establish a new one of taking responsibility.

Among all the habits eighteen year-olds bring into West Point, making excuses is perhaps the toughest to break. By the time we are eighteen, most of us have developed a world-class habit of making excuses. We learn to deflect responsibility for our failures by casting blame on circumstances and other people. At West Point, when an excuse came out of our mouths, the upper classmen were quick to correct us. We learned that voicing excuses is a weakness that would not be tolerated. Leaders are always responsible.

The excuses we made at eighteen are not very different from the ones people of all ages continue to use. What's worse is when it is a leader making these excuses. What follows are some excuses I (*The Business Guy*) hear in business settings. After each excuse is a response a Firstie (senior at West Point) would likely deliver.

A circumstance excuse: I would have been here on time, but I hit traffic on the way.

West Point Firstie: No excuse, Anderson! The traffic wasn't the issue. Your planning was. You did not leave enough cushion in case of traffic. Traffic is always a possibility. You did not plan for something that was a real possibility. That is your responsibility as a leader.

An other-people excuse: Sorry I am late, but my previous appointment started late.

West Point Firstie: No excuse, Anderson! Whose schedule is it? You made the schedule. You did not leave enough time between your meetings. By cutting it so close, you allowed this to happen. Your poor planning caused this, not your previous customer. Man up and own this. Be a leader.

There is not a West Point Firstie who would disagree with this statement: "Making excuses as a teenager is not acceptable. But making excuses as a leader is pathetic." The first time a cadet says, "No excuse, sir," it makes it easier to say the next time. Each time we said "No excuse, sir," we were developing a new habit. By the end of plebe year, cadets have shifted from making excuses to seizing responsibility.

When a leader can be counted on to do his *Duty* and take responsibility, a few things happen.

- When a mistake is made, the *Leader of Character* owns it without passing on blame. By not making excuses, the *Leader of Character* is trusted by his superiors, his peers, and his subordinates.
- When plan A or plan B fails, the *Leader of Character* does not look for circumstances or other people to explain away the failure. An excuse

is like a safety net. Without the safety net of an excuse, the *Leader of Character* persists with plan C, D, E, or F until a solution is found.

- When a team observes their leader taking ownership and persisting until the job is done or a solution is found, the *Leader of Character's* team develops the same can-do attitude the leader models.

Duty and Coaching

The *Leader of Character* knows it is her *Duty* as a leader to develop her people whether they like the process or not. She knows her level of comfort with the situation does not release her from the responsibility to add value to the people she leads. Just like a wise parent, the *Leader of Character* knows that to do what is best for the individual means that sometimes you must do something the individual will not like in the short-term. The *Leader of Character* believes it is her *Duty* to do what is necessary for the long-term growth of the individual. In other words, you are always working for the best interests of those you lead, even if it makes the other person or even you uncomfortable.

> Just like a wise parent, the *Leader of Character* knows that to do what is best for the individual means that sometimes you must do something the individual will not like in the short-term.

Many leaders avoid disciplining or even correcting individuals because it makes the leaders uncomfortable. The excuses some leaders make for not correcting a behavior are usually weak and self-centered: "The individual does not take criticism well"; "I don't want to have to deal with it"; "It's not worth the hassle." With these excuses and many others, we justify not actively stepping in and coaching, which indicates that our motivations are purely selfish. Those excuses expose our true motivations: we want to protect our own comfort level and convenience. Leaders who act or fail to act for such reasons reveal that they are more concerned about themselves than they are for their people.

A *Leader of Character* who has developed the habit of *Selflessness* may still be uncomfortable with having a tough conversation or may know that just having the conversation will slow down his day, but he will do his *Duty* anyway.

Duty and Setting the Example

The *Leader of Character* understands the saying, "More is caught than taught." There are no days off from leading. We influence people around us even when we are not trying to.

As young parents you learn quickly that your children are always watching you. And despite whatever you may tell them to do, they are much more likely to imitate your actions than they are to follow your words. This is also true for leaders at work. The words of a leader mean very little to his people if he does not model the behaviors he claims are important. If he tells his team that *Integrity* is a core value for the team and then instructs his assistant to tell someone that he is in a meeting when he is not, his actions will have more influence than any of his well-thought-out words.

It is our *Duty* to set the example for those we lead. And it doesn't matter if we are introverts or extroverts. Either can lead, and both kinds of personalities have a *Duty* to lead well. In fact, the actions of an introverted *Leader of Character* will lead a team to excellence before the eloquent words of a hypocritical extrovert.

As a *Leader of Character*, you must set the example in *Courage, Humility, Integrity, Selflessness, Duty,* and *Positivity* for everyone you are responsible for leading. Your *Duty* is that every choice you make as a leader is a choice between influencing people in a positive way or in a negative way. There is no middle ground. If you want to be a *Leader of Character*, you embrace the belief that it is your *Duty* to wield positive influence on everyone you meet.

Leaders of Character believe ...

- If I say I am going to do something, I will do it.
- If I say I will be somewhere at 10 a.m., I will be there.
- If I say I will complete a project by a particular date, I will complete it.

- If I see something that needs to be done, I will do it.
- If I can help someone improve, I will push them to grow.
- If I tell my kids I will be at their school play, I will be there.
- If I accept a paycheck from my employer, I will do my job to the best of my abilities.
- If I do not do the things listed above, I will own my failure, fix it, and do better next time.

Imagine what it would be like to be led by a person whose habits match the words in the box above. Who wouldn't want to be around a person with that sense of *Duty*? Who wouldn't want to follow that leader? Trust would never be a question, would it?

So how do you get there? How do you become that *Leader of Character* who has developed the habit of *Duty* to such a mature level? You start with the small choices: the smaller day-to-day decisions that help you form a *Habit of Character* that will prepare you for the larger tests. For instance, you pick up a random piece of trash on the street without giving it a second thought. You volunteer to complete a report for your boss when he is behind. You clean windows at home or do the dishes without expecting anything in return. You don't make excuses for your shortcomings. You don't try to manipulate reality so you do not have to own your mistakes. You accept the fact that you screwed up and that you need to do the work of finding solutions.

You do not give up, because you know that giving up is not doing your *Duty*. There is no excuse adequate enough to justify your giving up. You will not stop at plan A or B. You will find a way to persevere. You will go from plan A all the way to plan Z if need be in order to follow through on a commitment.

You coach everyone with an equal determination to make them better. You have difficult conversations when they are needed. You model the *Habits of Character* and understand people are paying more attention to your actions than to your words.

A *Leader of Character* is not selective when it comes to doing her *Duty*. She does it because she has developed it into a *Habit of Character* through intentional and consistent exercising of her *Duty* muscles. She breaks a sweat in practice so she is ready for game day.

> *"Duty is the sublimest word in the language; you can never do more than your duty; you shall never wish to do less."*
>
> **– Robert E. Lee**

Exercising *Duty*: Time to Break a Sweat

Duty is a *Habit of Character* just like the others we discussed. It is a habit formed over time. We all have a *Duty*. We have a *Duty* to our spouses, our children, our parents, our teams at work, our country, our environment, and our world. Exercising our *Duty* in one of these areas bleeds over into the others.

Each time we take action like the ones we have talked about in this chapter, it makes it easier for us to do the same thing the next time. As the weeks and months pass, we will find that we have stopped thinking about what our *Duty* is; instead our habits will have taken over and we will be doing our *Duty* without thinking about it. Our *Duty* will have become another facet of who we are.

Here are some exercises you can do to begin establishing *Duty* as one of your *Habits of Character*.

Overall

- ✓ Pick up newspapers or trash that the wind has brought into your field of sight from another home.
- ✓ Spend less on yourself and give more money away to others in need.
- ✓ Serve others without expecting anything in return.
- ✓ Count the number of excuses you make in a week, then cut it in half the next week, then again the following week.
- ✓ Volunteer to help our wounded veterans on a weekend when you'd rather be relaxing.
- ✓ Follow through on a commitment you wish you hadn't made.
- ✓ Don't keep score in any relationship.

At Work

- ✓ Stay late to complete a project that is behind because a co-worker did not complete her work on time.
- ✓ Coach the most difficult person on your team as passionately as you do your favorite person.
- ✓ Do the boring administrative parts of your job with excellence as if God himself were watching.
- ✓ End every conversation by asking others, "What do you need from me? How can I help you today?"

At Home

- ✓ Take the time to show your son or daughter how to change a tire, even though they may teach that in a driver's education course.
- ✓ With a smile on your face, do the thing you hate most.
- ✓ Call your mother-in-law even if you don't enjoy those conversations.
- ✓ Do a load of laundry for your wife even if she usually does that job.
- ✓ Take out the trash for your husband even if he usually does that.
- ✓ Teach your child the difference between an excuse and a reason, then work on modeling that in everything you do, especially at home.

Chapter 9

HABIT #6: POSITIVITY

The Warm-Up: Questions for Stretching Your Mind

Who is the most positive person you know? _____

How do you feel when you are around them? _____

On a scale of 1 to 10, with 1 being highly discouraged and 10 being highly encouraged, rate how people feel after they are with you?

Your co-workers _____ *, spouse* _____ *, and children* _____

The General's Story: *Women at West Point*

In 1976, I was involved with bringing the first women into West Point. As I look back at it now, I can't imagine any other experience that would require and develop the *Courage*, *Humility*, and *Positivity* those young women needed in order to graduate from West Point. They were there to become *Leaders of Character* and serve the common defense of our country, just like their male counterparts. But these women were the trailblazers. They were entering a historically male institution and were going to be expected to do something no woman had ever done before.

144

The US Congress wrote a law that prepared the way for the admission of women into the service academies. The initial version of the law required women to perform at the same level as the men for admission, retention, and graduation. There was never any doubt that women would be able to meet the academic requirements. However, there were real concerns about whether they could meet all of the physical requirements. We had done significant research on this and that contributed to our concerns.

When the proposed congressional bill arrived at West Point, it was sent to me for my comments. Based on our research, I argued that if Congress really meant for women to do everything the men were physically required to do, then very few, if any, women would graduate from West Point. I presented a solution I felt accomplished the goals of the bill and still gave young women a fair chance at succeeding while not compromising their readiness to be leaders in the US Army. I recommended that the bill be amended to add, "with minimum essential adjustments to account for physiological differences."

Congress accepted my recommendations, allowing me to make commonsense adjustments based on what our research showed. Those adjustments were based on what I thought were necessary to help the women cadets gain the same benefits that the men were receiving from their physical requirements.

To explain what I am talking about, let's look again at boxing. All of the male cadets at West Point are required to take boxing during their first (plebe) year. When I was preparing to become the professor and head of the Department of Physical Education by getting my doctorate, I knew that I was going to have to repeatedly explain why we required all male cadets to take boxing. This has been a requirement since before I was a cadet, and it continues today. The rationale for requiring the men to take boxing was to help them develop their *Courage*, self-confidence, and can-do attitude, all of which are required on the battlefield. I decided to test our assumptions in my PhD research. I was also interested in comparing boxing to some of the other physical activities, such as wrestling, gymnastics, and survival swimming.

The results of my doctoral dissertation showed that boxing did in fact have a significant impact on the self-concepts (*Courage*, confidence, and can-do attitude) of the male cadets, even for those who received failing grades at the end of the boxing classes. The other physical activities had no significant effect on the self-concepts of the male cadets.

In 1976, my commonsense told me that we should not require the women cadets to take boxing. Although boxing was an acceptable way for men to defend themselves, I do not think the same is true for women. If women need to defend themselves in combat, it would probably be against a man who is likely to be bigger, stronger, and more powerful. I did not think that trying to punch him out would be the most effective way if attacked.

That meant that we needed to find an alternative way for the women cadets to defend themselves and to develop their *Courage*, self-confidence, and can-do attitude as the men were doing in boxing. Therefore, we developed a self-defense course where women learned and competed against other women cadets in their first year. But in their second year, we felt that they needed to learn how the self-defense techniques worked when their opponent was a man. Men and women took a course together in close-quarters-combat during their sophomore year. In that class, the women competed against the men in realistic close-quarters combat scenarios. In the final exam, which we called "City Streets," both the men and women were attacked walking through blacked-out hallways. Bodies were flipped, punches were thrown, and attackers were disarmed while instructors graded the participants' responses.

The evidence that we collected indicated that the self-defense and close-quarters-combat courses did the same for the women that boxing did for the men. In other words, they were able to develop their *Courage*, self-confidence, and can-do attitude they would need to be *Leaders of Character* in the military.

The graduating class of 2020 at West Point will mark the 40th West Point class that includes women. All of the young women entering the academy over the last nearly forty years have raised their hands and said, "Send me." The *Courage, Humility, Integrity, Selflessness, Duty,* and *Positivity* new female cadets have demonstrated each summer since 1976 should be celebrated and is a great indication of the type of candidates West Point attracts.

Thanks to their can-do attitude on that first day and the character development process West Point asks all cadets to go through, women are now being commissioned into the United States Army through West Point as *Leaders of Character* prepared to serve the common defense. Taking the oath to defend the United States that first hot day in July in 1976 is an incredible example of the *Positivity* the trailblazers of the graduating class of 1980 exuded from day one.

Recently, three women officers who graduated from West Point became the first women to successfully complete the US Army Ranger School. I was an instructor at that school. I can assure you that no one, regardless of their gender, will successfully complete Ranger School if they do not demonstrate *Positivity*. By displaying a positive, can-do attitude under all circumstances in Ranger school, those three women are now the trailblazers for the coming generations of women in the Army.

The Business Guy's Story:
A Business Lesson from Elementary School

When my twins were in elementary school, I often coached their sports teams: soccer, basketball, and flag football. After elementary school, other coaches in middle school and high school took over. That's when I became a fan, sitting in the stands with the other parents and students.

As a coach and fan, I noticed one thing that is similar between seven-year-old and seventeen-year-old athletes. On any given day, someone will show up and not feel like playing. They will mope. They will play in the dirt. They will daydream. When the game finally begins, they may watch the ball go by them and only give a minimal effort. For whatever reason, on that particular day, that young athlete is not motivated to do anything. This happens at all age levels.

So what happens next? Usually the coach will pull the affected athlete aside and have a heart-to-heart conversation. These days most coaches are very encouraging in the early years while becoming more stern as the child gets older. After the conversation, the coach and the crowd usually see a new kid on the field. He is running around the field like a madman. He's sprinting, playing offense and defense, and making a major contribution to the team.

What brought about this dramatic change? The sport didn't change. The game, day, coach, and teammates are the same. And yet, the disengaged kid is playing his heart out. What changed? His attitude! He made a choice to change his attitude.

"Your attitude is a choice. Make a different choice." This was a stern comment I heard from *The General* at some point (and probably more than once) during high school. I never really thought about the comment until I started to examine how bad attitudes affected the workplace and my kids' sports teams.

Our attitudes are choices. We have the choice in the attitude we display. We all can make a different choice if we find ourselves complaining like Eeyore in the *Winnie the Pooh* books. If a seven-year-old can change his attitude on a soccer field, any adult reading this book can make the same choice as well. *Positivity* is a choice.

Defining *Positivity*

Too many people believe that they are not in control of their bad moods. They act like their moods are some uncontrollable tempest that takes over. Because they are not in control of their moods—maybe they got in a fight with their spouse or the air conditioning went out in the night or they simply woke up on the wrong side of the bed—they walk around as if it is everyone else's problem for getting in their way that day. It is our bad luck for running into them, so we are somehow responsible for dealing with their bad mood. This is self-indulgent garbage. The idea that other people must deal with us at our worst and we are entitled to behave terribly is a lie we tell ourselves at some of our most selfish moments.

Some people are focused on the reasons something won't succeed because they are bogged down by their attitudes toward their past. The past is often used as an excuse for finding a reason something will not work. *Positivity*, *Selflessness*, and *Duty* intersect here. When we eliminate a selfish focus and believe it is our *Duty*, our moral obligation, to find a way to make something work, we tend to see the possibilities.

The negative attitudes we hold onto put us in a position to predetermine our excuses for failure. As we stated in the chapter on *Duty*, if we believe there are no excuses for failure, we tend to persevere until we find a solution to a problem. We believe there is a way to get the job done; we just have not found it yet. When Plan A or B do not work, *Positivity* takes over and we continue to work until we find a solution, even if it takes getting to Plan Z! We develop a can-do attitude that becomes a *Habit of Character* and infuses the people around us with *Positivity*.

Andersons' 12-Word (or less) Definition of Positivity
Displaying a positive and/or can-do attitude in all circumstances

---

Common synonyms for *Positivity*: eagerness,
positiveness, zeal, readiness, confidence

What are some examples of people who choose to have *Positivity* in every circumstance?

- The woman unable to conceive children, who serves joyfully in the children's ministry every Sunday at church, taking care of other people's children.
- The cancer patient who lights up everyone else's day with positive comments and life wisdom.
- The mother who lost her child in the war on terrorism and mentors young mothers.
- The man who lost the business he built to a crooked partner but enthusiastically begins another business venture.

These are all examples of people who have more than enough reason to be angry or sad. Instead they choose not to behave that way. They made the choice not to allow their circumstances or other people to decide their attitudes about life. Despite everything, they have chosen to act like they are owed nothing and are blessed in every circumstance. They are not focused on what they believe they deserve today, but on possibilities of the future and what they can give others.

Just like the seven-year-old on the soccer field. Just like the woman who can't conceive. Just like the cancer patient. Just like the mother who lost her son. Each of us has a choice everyday. "Will I choose negativity, or will I choose *Positivity* today?"

None of us can control our circumstances or the behaviors of the people around us. But each one of us does have control over our attitude each and every day. Each time we choose to act like we are owed nothing and that we are blessed in all circumstances, it makes it easier for us to choose *Positivity* again. Conversely, each time we choose to wallow in negativity, it becomes easier for us to make that choice again as well.

Focus on the Possibilities

Our view of our current world affects how we see the future. When we are in the habit of looking at the world and our circumstances through the lens of self, we tend to see everything in a negative light.

Positivity comes down to our choices. Do we choose to see things through our self-focused lens or through the lens of *Positivity*? Do we choose to see the downside and the potential for failure in our circumstances, or do we see the possibilities, eliminate excuses, and move forward with *Positivity*? The choice is ours—every single day.

The Choice: Negativity or *Positivity*

A good attitude does not require me to think
less of myself but to think of myself LESS.

Bad attitudes stem from a place of self-pity. Pity is one of the most noble emotions there is—when we focus it outwardly. But when we turn pity on ourselves, it becomes self-pity, which is one of the most ignoble emotions available to any of us.

The elevation of self above others—when we believe our rights, our desires, or our needs are most important—is a reflection of the lack of other *Habits of Character*: *Humility* and *Selflessness*. And self-pity puts us ahead of others.

The people we cited above refused to wallow in self-pity, even though most of us would likely agree that they had every reason to do so. If we truly spent time evaluating what we encounter everyday, most of us would realize that our troubles—the things that cause us to go into the pit of despair and self-pity—

pale in comparison to these people who reached out beyond themselves to help others instead of turning inward in self-pity. Nevertheless, at times we still tend to throw pity parties for ourselves.

Pity Parties

We all have seen a pity party, and they are not pretty! Have you ever tried to talk someone out of their pity party? As they linger in that pit of despair and self-pity, you begin to point out the positives in their lives or in the situation they are moping about.

"Hey, at least you didn't lose your job."

"Your kids are still great and none of them are in trouble."

"Your spouse is making plenty of money to support your family during your transition."

"You have a lot of marketable skills."

"You know a lot of people who will lend you a hand."

You keep laying out the many positives in their lives, but the person having the pity party can't see any of them. "But you don't understand …," they say.

Self-pity creates an incapacity inside most of us that clouds reality. We cannot see beyond our own self-pity to see what everyone else sees as true about our situation. Our thoughts and therefore our personal reality become distorted.

If we choose to allow these thoughts to take hold too often, we will develop an awful habit. We will become a joy sucker. All we will see are the negatives in every situation. The belief that we are entitled to more while ignoring what we have will keep us self-focused to our detriment and that of those around us.

Joy Suckers

The entitlement mentality that pervades our culture creates the joy suckers we run into daily. The joy suckers do not add anything to anyone. Joy suckers subtract from those around them. Whenever a joy sucker walks into a room, everyone else walks out feeling worse.

Have you ever run into a joy sucker? You wake up to a beautiful, sunny day after a good night's sleep. Your spouse and kids have slept well too. You have a Norman Rockwell type of breakfast together before getting in the car to drive to work. On the way to the office, you hit every green light and not a single driver cuts you off.

When you get to the office, no one is waiting to unload an issue on you, and your morning calendar shows no unnecessary meetings are scheduled. With a big sigh and a great outlook for the day, you head to the break room to get a cup of coffee. When you get there you see one other person in the room. It is Tony, and unfortunately he sees you. You can't turn and run, so you walk in and cheerfully say, "Good morning, Tony! How's it going?"

Fifteen minutes later, you walk out of the break room worn out and in a bad mood. Tony succeeded in dragging you into his pit of despair and self-pity. The day that started out so well is a distant memory.

Attitudes are contagious! Is yours worth catching? Tony's isn't, and his bad attitude infected you just like your negativity infects others.

One person with a bad attitude can drag down everyone they encounter. If it is someone inside the team, that is bad enough. But if the leader is the joy sucker who focuses on the negative or what can't be done, that team or family will rarely move forward. Joy suckers are great at ruining your day, no matter how well it started out.

The other side of the coin are those people who never seem to have a bad day. They are that tall cool glass of water on a hot summer day. Every time you are around them, you feel better. When you are down about your circumstances, they point you toward the possibilities in your life. They lift you up without even seeming to try. When such a person walks away from you, you think, *Wow! She was great!* That one person with *Positivity* can change your day, even make it soar.

What are we going to be for others? *Who* are we going to be for others? Are we going to be the joy sucker who subtracts from everyone he meets? Or are we going to be the tall cool glass of water that refreshes and adds to others? Are we going to help people see the negative side of every situation or the possibilities? Are we going to model the can-do attitude that promotes *Positivity,* or the can't-do-anything model that upholds negativity?

Encourager or discourager? Joy giver or joy sucker? Ms. Positive or Ms. Negative? The choice is ours.

Encourager or discourager? Joy giver or joy sucker?
Ms. Positive or Ms. Negative? The choice is ours.

Negativity Versus *Positivity*

Negativity: Choosing to consistently focus on why a new idea won't work.
Positivity: Choosing to find reasons a new idea will work before poking holes in it.

Negativity: Choosing to focus on what could go wrong in every situation.
Positivity: Choosing to see the possibilities instead of the limitations.

Negativity: Choosing to focus on your own past failures and those of others.
Positivity: Choosing to forgive yourself and others and move forward.

Negativity: Choosing to see a negative motive in most people.
Positivity: Choosing to trust others until they prove untrustworthy.

Negativity: Choosing to snicker at the excitement of others and call them naïve.
Positivity: Choosing to harness the excitement of others and move it toward a realistic solution.

Negativity: Choosing to tell children their goals are not realistic.
Positivity: Choosing to encourage their dreams and help them see the hard work that will be needed to accomplish a worthwhile dream.

Most people do not want to spend time with a joy sucker. They drain you and make your days worse.

Some people would call a joy sucker a pessimist. When you tell someone she is a pessimist, her favorite retort is often "I am not a pessimist, I am a realist." To that we say that the only time pessimists are optimists is when they call themselves realists!

The only time pessimists are optimists is when they call themselves realists!

Whatever you call yourself, many of us choose negativity over *Positivity*. Whether we find *Positivity* easy or not does not mean we are stuck with our current disposition. Both *Positivity* and negativity are choices, and either can become a habit when we reinforce it regularly.

We need to begin to behave differently by thinking differently. We need to change our thoughts about what we are entitled to in life. One of the best ways to beat entitlement is thankfulness. We need to begin being thankful for all that we have instead of focusing on all we feel entitled to having. Both entitlement and thankfulness are habits too.

We change habits one new decision at a time. Each time we make a choice to be thankful, it makes it easier to make that same choice again. All habits are formed this way.

Our character is revealed based on our view of the circumstances we start with. Do we start by looking for the downside or by looking at the possibilities? Do we start by looking at how something may affect us, or do we look at it based on how it will help others? Do we start from a position of entitlement or from a position of thankfulness for what we have? *Positivity* starts with seeing the possibilities and being thankful because we believe we are not entitled to anything.

Positivity and *Leaders of Character*

Imagine walking into a party and you only know two people there. If one is the Debbie Downer, the joy sucker, the one who oozes negativity, and the other person is someone you can count on to be positive and uplifting, who do you want to speak with? Who do you gravitate towards? Leaders attract followers the same way. If you want to lead others, if you want to be a *Leader of Character* who attracts people instead of chasing them away, your *Positivity* is key.

Leaders of Character have an infectious attitude that everybody wants. Like everyone else, *Leaders of Character* have bad days. However, they choose not to let their bad days infect other people. *Leaders of Character* also face obstacles as others do. But they choose not to let those obstacles prevent them from finding another way to succeed. They choose *Positivity* in all circumstances. This is the attitude toward life they embrace—no matter what. A *Leader of Character* asks himself this: *Attitudes are contagious! Is mine worth catching?*

Positivity and the Past

There are plenty of people in this world who have ugly pasts, but they refuse to allow their pasts to turn them into pessimists. They have chosen to approach life differently, learning from their past but not choosing to let their past decide their present or future outlook. We, *The General* and *The Business Guy*, have encountered many such people, including these:

- A cancer patient who sees nothing but possibilities.
- A man whose wife died in a car accident yet believes in his future.
- A man who was abused in his childhood and now works selflessly with kids who are going through similar circumstances.
- A Ugandan woman whose husband passed HIV on to her and then left her with four kids to raise. She never stops smiling and now cares for six more children at an orphans' home near Kampala.

A pessimist's view of these same situations is understandable. These are serious and heartbreaking situations. On the other hand, these examples— which we can multiply many times over—prove that we all have a choice. *Positivity* and *Selflessness* are not easy choices to make, but these people have made the tough choices, even though their circumstances were much worse than many of us have faced.

Most of us have an easier choice to make than these people have. And our choice concerning how we deal with our past affects our outlook on life and our attitude toward it. If we choose to stay wrapped up in the things that went wrong in the past, we will never get past them.

If because of your past, you are in the habit of seeing the negative in most situations, you are less and less likely to try anything new. Because of this, pessimists tend to stay where they are in life, failing to grow as the rest of the world moves forward. As bad as this is, it affects more than the person who chooses to stagnate. All of us impact the lives of the people we come in contact with. The people we work and live with tend to be moved forward or held back by our attitudes. Pessimists generally hold people back while optimists usually move people forward. What kind of person do you want to be? Do you want to help or hinder? Do you want to be the kind of leader people love to follow or the kind people want to avoid?

> The people we work and live with tend to be moved forward
> or held back by our attitudes. Pessimists generally hold
> people back while optimists usually move people forward.

If your attitude toward your past is holding you and those around you back, you need to see your past in a new light, use it in a new way—a way that inspires rather than repels.

This does not mean experience doesn't matter or that a *Leader of Character* when he hears a bad idea, ignores the red flags that fly inside of him. Experience is an asset that helps us make wiser choices. It just means he must look at bad ideas through a different lens. It means he needs to address those bad ideas in a different way. Instead of saying why something won't work, we need to start by saying, "It would be even better if ...." This approach leads leaders and followers to look for a better solution rather than just shut down the proposed one. It also allows the problem-solving process to continue. If as a leader you stifle this process by only identifying flaws in proposed solutions, you also squash opportunities for success. Leaders and followers need to work toward better solutions rather than just shooting down proposed answers.

It is a leader's job to move the team forward. A leader who holds the team back due to his negative attitude is not a *Leader of Character*. The *Leader of Character* has developed the *Habit of Character* called *Positivity*. He does not let his past disappointments influence his current attitude. He is able to overcome the past because he does not feel entitled to more and feels blessed by what he does have.

Positivity and Thankfulness

It is amazing what can happen to a person's attitude after she spends time with less fortunate people groups. *The General* spent two tours in Vietnam, and *The Business Guy* served in Iraq and served on a short-term mission trip to Uganda. We both came away from our overseas experience amazed by the *Positivity* of the people we met in those countries. When we looked at the living conditions, and the pervasive disease and poverty that surrounded these people, we found their attitudes remarkable. They had so little yet were so joyful. While in our culture, we have so much, yet we are so joyless. They are content and thankful with what they have, while we feel we are entitled to more and are discouraged when we don't get it. Having *Positivity* does not mean we don't desire something more. It just means we do not believe we are entitled to more. If we can defeat entitlement, we can defeat negativity.

Having *Positivity* does not mean we don't desire something more.
It just means we do not believe we are entitled to more.

Practicing thankfulness may be the best weapon against entitlement. Spending time focused on what we have versus what we don't have changes our attitudes. At work, if we are thankful for the budget we have, the personnel we have, and the equipment we have, we can accomplish much. With *Positivity*, people focus on succeeding with what they have instead of setting up excuses for failure unless they get more. This same lesson works at home as well. If we train ourselves and our families to focus on the blessings we have versus the desires that are not being met, thankfulness overtakes entitlement and *Positivity* reigns. Our families learn that their positive attitudes towards what they have will take them further than the unquenchable desire to attain more ever will.

> *"A people that values its privileges above its principles soon loses both."*
> – **Dwight D. Eisenhower**

Positivity and Getting Things Done

In 2015, the first female graduates of the Army's Ranger School set an example for all of us for *Positivity* and getting things done. They overcame unique obstacles as trailblazers in what has been an all-male enterprise. Plus, they overcame the traditional obstacles that have stopped generations of would-be male Rangers from earning the title of Army Ranger. This accomplishment, like many worthwhile accomplishments for any leader, would not have been possible without having the right attitude—*Positivity*. A *Leader of Character* must develop the habit of believing in the possibilities and her ability to overcome the obstacles that life, circumstances, and other people may throw in her path.

One way a *Leader of Character* develops this can-do attitude is by pushing himself outside his current boundaries, whatever they may be. If we only operate within the boundaries of our past or current experiences, new obstacles will become our focus instead of envisioning the possibilities that will open up by overcoming those obstacles. *Courage* is required to face these obstacles, and *Positivity* allows us to see beyond the obstacles and focus on the desired outcome.

We must have the *Courage* to push ourselves to do hard things if we want to grow beyond the person we currently are. A *Leader of Character* sees that pushing herself through or finding a way around the obstacles in life is when she is most likely to see growth. *Positivity* means we don't believe growth occurs in comfort. Therefore, if something is uncomfortable or difficult, we see it as an opportunity, not as a looming failure. When we focus on the desired outcome, the obstacles become challenges to be solved instead of predictors of failures that prevent us from moving forward. In other words, when a *Leader of Character* has a door slam in her face, she kicks open a window.

A *Leader of Character* also understands that it is his *Duty* to get things done. Therefore he does not leave himself the option of making excuses for failure. Without that option, the attitude becomes "This can be done; we just haven't found the right way to do it yet."

By choosing to look at our past through a different lens, by choosing thankfulness instead of entitlement, and by choosing to get things done instead of standing still, we develop the habit of *Positivity* that changes our trajectory in life and sets us up to be *Leaders of Character*. On top of that, if we model a positive attitude for our teams at work and our families at home, we create willing and eager followers instead of disengaged individuals just trying to survive. What group would you rather lead?

By the way, the pessimist reading this is probably saying, "Yeah, right. Nice drivel, guys." The *Leader of Character*, on the other hand, who has developed *Positivity* as a *Habit of Character*, is probably thinking about whom he can positively impact today and how he can make things happen. Who would you rather be? Who would you rather follow?

"Part of being an optimist is keeping one's head pointing toward the sun and one's feet moving forward."
– Nelson Mandela

Exercising *Positivity*: Time to Break a Sweat

Your attitude is a habit. Just like every character habit we have discussed, each time you make a choice to behave in a certain way, it makes it easier to behave that way again in the future. Each time you choose to let circumstances or other people determine your attitude, it makes it easier to do it again.

It is time to exercise. Your attitude may be out of shape. You may feel you are entitled to behave negatively. You may have let the unhealthy circumstances in your life have control over you. You may have stopped yourself or others from moving forward because you are unsure if it can be done. But to be a

Leader of Character, you have to get your attitude in shape. You have to start exercising *Positivity*.

Here's what you need to do. You have to focus on breaking your old habits—those that keep you focused on yourself, your circumstances, or the obstacles you face. You need to begin to develop new habits that help you see that you do not deserve any special treatment from the world, that things you already have are a blessing, and because something is hard does not mean it cannot or should not be done. So here are some exercises that develop *Positivity* and lead you away from negativity, being a joy sucker, and lead you toward the *Positivity* that is a habit for *Leaders of Character*.

Overall
- ✓ Make a list of everything you are thankful for in your life. Refer back to it often.
- ✓ Try something new that you are unsure you can accomplish.
- ✓ Come up with three reasons a new idea can work before verbalizing why it won't.
- ✓ Say "even better if …" when you hear an idea you are skeptical about.
- ✓ Start each week by making a list of the positives from the week before.
- ✓ Leave everyone you encounter feeling better about themselves.
- ✓ Turn a conversation with a joy sucker to a positive discussion.
- ✓ Accomplish something others believe you are not capable of doing.
- ✓ Do not give up. Find a new way.

At Work
- ✓ Choose to leave your bad mood in the car before you walk into work.
- ✓ Encourage someone to try something new to solve a problem.
- ✓ Celebrate positive accomplishments publicly.
- ✓ Leave everyone you speak to at work with a positive word.
- ✓ Coach a joy sucker to identify three reasons a new idea could work before he verbalizes his concerns about the idea.
- ✓ Instead of starting with why something won't work, ask, "Can you help me understand your thought process on this?"

At Home

- ✓ Choose to leave your bad mood in the car before you walk in the house.
- ✓ Encourage your spouse or your child to do something new and difficult.
- ✓ Help your spouse or child create a plan for reaching a difficult goal.
- ✓ Encourage big goals from your family members.
- ✓ Never let your family see you give up when things get tough.
- ✓ Do not let your child quit a sport mid season when things get hard or he or she isn't getting playing time.
- ✓ Teach and model giving maximum effort with a cheerful attitude.

PART 4

DO WHAT YOU
WANT TO BE

Chapter 10

WHERE ARE TODAY'S
LEADERS OF CHARACTER?

You become "just by doing just acts ... you become brave by doing brave acts, you learn virtue by following rules of good behavior, hearing stories of virtuous people, and imitating virtuous models."
 — Aristotle, *Nicomachean Ethics*

We began our discussion of character with the teaching of Aristotle, so it seems appropriate to follow him to the end. While we have pointed out the problems in our leadership development efforts in our culture, we want to be sure to highlight some cases where *Leaders of Character* are being developed successfully and changing our culture as a result. These are the virtuous people and virtuous models Aristotle says we should emulate. They are today's examples that we should hold in high respect and strive to imitate.

Female Army Rangers: Today's *Leaders of Character*

In August 2015, a landmark shift occurred in the United States Army. The Army's elite Ranger School graduated its first two female Rangers. A month later a third woman graduated. All soldiers entering Ranger School are always vetted and determined to be some of the best soldiers the Army has to offer. But despite that vetting, through the decades the historically all-male Ranger School has averaged a 60 percent failure rate among male soldiers. How would the women do in such a tough environment? In April 2015, the Ranger School was about to find out. Nineteen women stepped in to accept every challenge the school had to offer.

Just like the women who entered West Point in the summer of 1976, the nineteen women who started Ranger School in April 2015 walked in as trailblazers. Six of those nineteen women were graduates of West Point, but all of those who volunteered to challenge the status quo at Ranger School knew they were about to attempt something many people believed was impossible.

When it was all said and done, three of the women made it through the grueling training. In fact, only 30 percent of all the Ranger candidates who started with these three women completed the course. The three women, who were all West Point graduates, received the coveted Ranger Tab that many other male and female candidates were unable to earn. Over the years many thousands of entering Rangers tried but never received that honor as well.

Why did these women make it through, while the other sixteen women did not? For many of the same reasons some men make it through while others do not. While Ranger School is physically demanding, its rigor is ultimately a challenge of the *Habits of Character* we have been talking about. Without *Courage, Humility, Integrity, Selflessness, Duty,* and *Positivity,* few people, regardless of their gender, will ever make it through the school's training challenges.

West Point is a unique training environment for character. While three other women and many men from West Point did not make it through Ranger School, we believe the three female Rangers were well prepared for the challenge because of their training at West Point. All six of the *Habits of Character* are challenged and developed during a cadet's four-year stay at the academy. When a West Point graduate becomes a Ranger candidate, he or she already has four years of training focused on developing their *Courage, Humility, Integrity, Selflessness, Duty,* and *Positivity.*[8]

---

8   Although West Point does not formally teach the virtue of *Humility* to its students, many cadets leave West Point with a sense of *Humility* about them, as we mentioned in chapter 5. While we applaud that outcome, we still believe that *Humility* should be part of the formal discussions on leadership so all cadets have a better opportunity of developing it while they go through their courses and other training.

Talking or reading about these *Habits of Character* did not get these women through Ranger School. Nor was it the classroom education about honor and *Integrity* that prepared them for the unique challenge they faced. Instead, the key for them, and for all *Leaders of Character,* was that they practiced! They knew they had to DO what they wanted to BE. They worked hard to develop the *Habits of Character* in the smaller challenges that West Point provided so that they were ready for the larger challenges facing them at Ranger School.

So who were the women who graduated from Ranger School? One was Captain Kristen Griest of the Military Police. She also finished fourth among all Ranger candidates and first in her company on the infamous twelve-mile forced march (Ruck). Another was First Lieutenant Shaye Hauer, an Apache Helicopter Pilot. The third was Major Lisa Jaster, who completed the course as a thirty-seven-year-old mother of two children. She was also an invaluable resource to us as we endeavored to tell their story with accuracy.

These are the three Rangers who accomplished something that could not have been done unless they had developed the *Habits of Character* every US Army Ranger needs in order to become an elite soldier and a *Leader of Character*.

The following comments from classmates, instructors, and the graduates themselves illustrate that these three women are *Leaders of Character* and role models for both women and men who aspire to be *Leaders of Character* themselves, no matter where they serve.

- **Ranger classmate on *Courage, Integrity,* and *Duty after Griest and Hauer graduation***

"We are universally in awe of what these two female graduates have accomplished. Everyone (other Ranger classmates) I've talked to are of one mind. They earned it."
    – Ranger Rudy Mac, Ranger class, June 2015

- **Brigade Command Sergeant Major at Airborne and Ranger Training Brigade on *Duty* and *Positivity after Griest and Hauer graduation***

"These two soldiers have absolutely earned the respect of every Ranger Instructor. They did not quit and they did not complain."
  – Command Sergeant Major Curtis Arnold

• **Female Ranger School graduate on *Courage, Humility,* and *Positivity***

"I hope they (future women) come with a strong mind. I couldn't be more proud and humbled by the experience."
  – Ranger 1LT Shaye Hauer, Ranger class, August 2015

• **Female Ranger School graduate on *Selflessness* and *Duty***

"I was thinking of the future generations of women, so I had that pressure on myself."
  – Ranger Captain Kristen Griest, Ranger class, August 2015

• **Female Ranger School graduate on *Courage, Humility, Integrity, Selflessness, Duty,* and *Positivity***

"The right way includes being professional, thick skinned, and ensuring that we minimize any special treatment. I know that I am physically fit. I am mentally tough. I know that I have all the ingredients to be successful. I volunteered because I want to make sure the standards do remain high and that women coming out at the far end of Ranger School will be respected for their accomplishments rather than being judged for making things easier."
  – Ranger Major Lisa Jaster, Ranger class, September 2015

The women graduates of the Army Ranger School are *Leaders of Character.* They set an example for soldiers and civilians alike by exercising the *Habits of Character* in order to prepare them for the test the Army Ranger School provided.

The *Leaders of Character* we need today can be found in many different walks of life. They can be found at elite military universities and at hardcore combat leadership schools such as West Point and the Ranger School. But the key to being a *Leader of Character* does not come from being in the military. The key is knowing what makes a *Leader of Character* and then putting in the effort in everyday life to develop the strength we will need when our character is challenged in the big things.

Express Employment Professionals (Express): Today's *Company of Character*

Can companies founded on character continue to grow and be successful without losing the values or culture that made them great? Express Employment Professionals is a *Company of Character* led by a *Leader of Character* that is doing just that. Express began in 1983. It is a privately owned franchise organization. It has grown from a locally owned business based in Oklahoma to having more than 745 locations in the United States, Canada, and South Africa with over $2.85 billion in annual revenue.

Express Employment Professionals' Mission Statement is "To help as many people as possible find great jobs and help as many businesses as possible find great people." CEO Bob Funk was at the helm in 1983 and continues to lead his company with character after more than thirty years.

As of the writing of this book, I (*The Business Guy*) have worked with Express Employment Professionals and experienced the culture of the company for more than three years.

The Character of Express Employment Professionals

Courage, Integrity, and Duty

Bob Funk believes that his company's most important character qualities are *Integrity* and professionalism (*Duty*). He says they never lost focus on their *Integrity* and their responsibilities to their franchisees. "Whatever we said we would do, we would do for our franchisees. At times we did double and triple what we said we would do in our franchise agreements. Even if at financial sacrifice to the company .... You have to have the *Courage* to do the right thing."[9]

---

9   This quote from Bob Funk and the others from him in this section are taken from an interview that aired on IMPACT Talk Radio on January 13, 2016. (Podcast available on iTunes or http://toginet.com/shows/impacttalkradio.

For Express, professionalism (*Duty*) means "treat others as we would want to be treated and be the best in the industry that we can possibly be." They do not stop at doing what is required of them. They strive to over-deliver to their customers and their franchise owners. This was a constant when they had just ten franchises and continues today with 745 franchises.

Humility, Selflessness, and Positivity

Bob and his leadership team do something few executives claim to have time to do as a company grows: they listen. Virtually every week they bring in owners and employees and ask for feedback and suggestions on improving. Bob says, "You have to be willing to accept criticism." To ask for and accept criticism from all comers requires *Humility, Selflessness,* and *Positivity*. That's especially true for any leader, let alone a CEO of a multi-billion dollar company.

Bob believes, "We have to love people enough to want them to achieve more than you achieve." The most strikingly unique aspect of Express is the *Humility* and *Selflessness* evident at the company's annual International Leadership Conference (ILC). Every year more than fifteen hundred company leaders join together to celebrate the past year's achievements, set goals for the new year, and participate in a variety of training opportunities. As do most CEOs, Bob is inundated with meetings. But perhaps his favorite meeting is the ILC. Bob has been known to warn newly hired executives, "I guarantee you, you will get more hugs this week than any other week in your life." The atmosphere is more like a family reunion than a corporately sponsored junket. Hugs abound at ILC as do impromptu moments of prayer where people stop and demonstrate that they care for one another by taking the time to pray.

In fact, Express annually has a voluntary prayer breakfast that people wake up for an hour early to attend. During this time together, people share personal and professional challenges and also give thanks for the obstacles they've overcome in the past twelve months. Bob boldly proclaims, "This comes from being faith-based. We are selfless because Christ set the example for us, and we as leaders try to set that same example." It serves as a bonding time between the leaders and the led as they acknowledge their challenges together and demonstrate that "We are in this together." The prayer breakfast is standing-room-only year after year.

These ILC meetings are a snapshot of the culture that Bob and his leadership team began in 1983. For a smaller company, this may not be unique. But for a company doing business and growing like Express is, it is amazing. The time they take to celebrate the success of the past and care for those who are struggling in the present demonstrates a *Humility* and *Selflessness* at the top of the organizational chart that permeates the company's culture, whether it be in Oklahoma City, Chicago, or Johannesburg.

Maintaining Character While Growing

But how did Express maintain a family atmosphere where values like *Courage, Humility, Integrity, Selflessness, Duty,* and *Positivity* define the company's character? It comes down to communication and focus. The values are communicated through words and actions at every level. Leaders walk the walk and talk the talk, and they do not accept anyone on the team who does not share those values.

It takes more than business savvy to become an Express franchise owner. The company received over eight thousand inquiries in the last twelve months and awarded only seventy-five people franchises. The number one factor for Express is the character of each potential owner. If that person does not have the *Habits of Character* that Express Employment Professionals holds as standards, then he or she will not be awarded a franchise.

> *"Character builds loyalty. It is a two-way street. If you are loyal to them, they will be loyal to the company. That takes character."*
> **– Bob Funk**

Express Employment Professionals is a great example of what Fred Kiel calls "Return on Character." Not only are the financial results incredible, but also the intangible results are priceless. You have to DO what you want to BE! Express Employment Professionals began in 1983 and continues doing what they need to DO to become the company they want to BE—a *Company of Character.*

Chapter 11

JOIN THE NEW COUNTERCULTURE

You have to DO what you want to BE!

Leadership is a blend of competence and character. Many well-meaning schools, training departments, management consultants, and leadership authors spend an incredible amount of time focused on the development of our management competence. That's why we did not add to that ever-growing list of competency-based resources.

As we stated from the start, our goal is to get each of you to realize that your character is why people follow you. Your character is why they will trust you, believe in you, and will respond to your direction and coaching. Your character is what will take a group of compliant rule followers and turn them into a committed and motivated team. But to develop the character side of leadership, you have to DO the things *Leaders of Character* do to BE a *Leader of Character*.

Now you stand at a crossroad. You can finish reading these last few pages and change nothing. Or you can stop reading now, put this book on the shelf with the other leadership books you have read, and move forward with your life on the same course as it was before. Or you can do something different, something far better.

***To accomplish things we have never accomplished before,
we have to start doing things we have never done before.***

Character Development: How It Works

- Our character starts with our *thoughts*.
- Our thoughts influence our *words*.
- Our words lead us to our *actions*.
- Our actions, repeated over time, become our *habits*.
- Our habits form our *character*.

We designed our book to help you follow the character development model detailed in chapter 3. You have read this far, and maybe even read certain chapters more than once. That is a great first step (*thoughts*).

The next step is to let people know about your new leadership workout plan. Tell them what you are trying to improve upon. You can also share this book with others and hold each other accountable to sticking with your workouts (*words*).

But just reading and talking about working out will not get you in shape. You have to begin performing the exercises (*actions*).

When you make the choice to exercise a certain muscle, it makes it easier to make that choice again. Over time, you will begin to make that choice without thinking (*habit*).

By regularly exercising, strengthening your weak muscles and maintaining your stronger ones, you will become healthy (*character*).

When we are willing and able to do the things we have never done before, we end up accomplishing things we have never accomplished before. We become different people. If you follow our character development plan, you will change—and you will change for the better.

The question now is, do you want to BE a *Leader of Character*? If your answer is yes, then you must DO what *Leaders of Character* do and that is exercise your *Courage, Humility, Integrity, Selflessness, Duty,* and *Positivity.*

You may still be wondering, "What's in it for me?" We get it. The workouts we laid out in this book require sacrifice. They ask you to be different than the person you have been. They ask you to do things no one else is doing and to do them on a regular basis. These workouts ask you to go against our culture. Being countercultural will make others question what happened to the old you. But if you want to be a *Leader of Character*, that won't bother you. In fact, making this decision may be an exercise in developing your habit of *Courage*.

Being a *Leader of Character* may be countercultural and hard to do, but it has its benefits, some tangible and others not. The tangible benefits are spelled out in Fred Kiel's groundbreaking book *Return on Character: The Real Reason Leaders and Their Companies Win*. Kiel's consulting group, KRW International, looked at eighty-four CEOs and did extensive research into the character of those leaders. The group's work with them included interviews with the leaders and the people they led. What Kiel's group found was that the *Leaders of Character* (what they called "Virtuoso Leaders") had financial results five times better than the "Self-Focused" CEOs. Kiel also made some observations about these Virtuoso Leaders that support the *Leader of Character* workout plans you have been reading about:

- *Leaders of Character* are rarely driven by fears. (*Courage*)
- *Leaders of Character* are more self-aware. They spend time reflecting on who they are and learning from their past. (*Humility*)
- *Leaders of Character* stand up for what is right and keep their promises. (*Integrity*)
- *Leaders of Character* are committed to the development of their people. (*Duty*)
- *Leaders of Character* put the success and welfare of other people ahead of their own concerns. (*Selflessness*)
- *Leaders of Character* focus on what is right with the world and it's possibilities. (*Positivity*)

The bottom line of Kiel's extensive research is that *Leaders of Character* produce tangible results. If results are what companies want, his research should drive companies to find and develop *Leaders of Character* in their midst.

As advantageous as the tangible benefits are, the intangible benefits of becoming a *Leader of Character* are even more profound and impactful. Becoming a *Leader of Character* changes lives—our lives and the lives of the people we touch. Our lives are the most effective leadership tool available. The thousands of witnesses to this include our coworkers, employees, friends, spouses, and children, all of who are watching how we live our lives more than listening to what we have to say. What we do on a habitual basis is more of a statement about who we are than any well-crafted message we may deliver to those observing our lives.

How will I be remembered? What will be my legacy? These are good questions. And when we ask them, we should realize that most people will remember us mostly for who we are:

- Bob stood up for me when no one else would. (*Courage*)
- Sarah was the first to admit when she was wrong. She knew she was not perfect. (*Humility*)
- He was my best friend because I knew he would tell me the truth about myself, even if it hurt. (*Integrity*)
- My husband served our family and me without ever grumbling. (*Selflessness*)
- Caroline gave everything her all and never blamed others for her shortcomings. (*Duty*)
- Mom had a contagious attitude that left everyone feeling better about themselves. (*Positivity*)

Only you know what kind of shape your character is in. If you want an unbiased look at yourself, don't forget you can take an online assessment here: http://alslead.com/character-test. You may find yourself stronger in the areas of *Humility* and *Selflessness* but weak in *Courage* or *Integrity*. That's alright. After all, none of us is a finished product. Our *Habits of Character* are always in need of maintenance. Even if you are strong in certain habits, you will become vulnerable by ignoring them and assuming they will always be strong. Just like a muscle you don't exercise, the habits that were once strong will grow weaker with neglect and will eventually fail you.

At the end of each chapter, we provided some specific exercises that will strengthen your weaker character muscles and maintain the fitness of the stronger ones. But whether you become a *Leader of Character* is ultimately in your hands. There are no quick answers to building your character, just like one week at the gym will not transform you into a Greek god or goddess. Becoming a *Leader of Character* takes practice and sweat. Like many of the world's greatest athletes and chefs, you won't get a lot of attention for the hard work you put in when no one is watching. But the tangible results you will get are real, and the intangible benefits are life changing for you and those you lead.

We, *The General* and *The Business Guy*, are committed to be there with you on this journey. Like you, we are exercising, we are learning, we are growing alongside of you. To get regularly updated, custom-designed *Leaders of Character* resources that will even take you beyond this book, check out our website: http://alslead.com. You can also contact us there and leave comments and questions for us. At alslead.com you can find free blogs and videos and links to other resources. You can also join our exclusive Leaders of Character Fitness Group. You will get access to exclusive character growth resources you can use for personal growth or with your teams and families.

The impact of this book and the exercise plans we provide on http://alslead.com depend on your willingness to work hard and break a sweat in order to become the *Leader of Character* your work teams, your families, and your nation needs. We do not want this book to be something you read once. Instead, we want it to be something you use to continue to develop as a *Leader of Character* throughout your life.

The solution for our culture's leadership crisis is not complicated, but it is hard to achieve. The solution to the leadership crisis does not lie in our training departments, our schools, or our governments. The solution is not more training on management skills or more leaders getting MBAs. We have to stop giving cough medicine to pneumonia patients. We need to treat the underlying cause that the symptoms are pointing toward, namely, *character*.

The solution to the leadership crisis lies in each of us who aspire to lead and to lead well. Remember that leadership hero we asked you to describe? Wouldn't you love to follow that person? Why is he or she your Leadership Hero? It probably has very little to do with the Hero's competence and everything to do with the Hero's character. *Character* is why you follow leaders and why people will follow you.

Andersons' 12-Word (or less) Definition of Character
Our habitual way of operating: HOW we are is WHO we are!

We have to look in the mirror and see ourselves for who we truly are.

What type of shape *is* our *Habits of Character* in? *Courage, Humility, Integrity, Selflessness, Duty,* and *Positivity* are the solution to our leadership crisis. The solution is *Leaders of Character,* and we can become those leaders by our willingness to do the hard work that will strengthen our *Habits of Character* so we will become the *Leaders of Character* God designed us to be.

Did you just hear Coach K blow his whistle? It's time to start practice again!

Character Assessment: http://alslead.com/character-test

Appendix A

Developing Families of Character

The most important place any of us are called to lead is in our homes. It does not matter if we are the CEO of a multi-billion dollar company or the owner of a small business. The legacy we leave at work pales in comparison with our legacy within our family. When we die, we will be replaced at work, in our golf foursomes, and anywhere we had volunteered. The only place we will not be replaced is in the hearts of our families. The question is, what sort of family are we leading? What can we do to be sure our family legacy is a legacy of character?

Knowing What We Stand For

Just like any organization, every family needs a set of values. The values in a family may not be on a website or on a poster in the break room, but all families would do well to determine what values they hold dear.

Values help organizations and families understand what is most important, what they believe and how they will behave. The time to figure that out is not in a crisis or in the face of temptation. We and our children need to be prepared before the crisis or the temptation comes. We are not born with values. They are instilled in us as we grow up. So who will instill those values in our children? Will it be those of us who are their parents? Will it be their teachers or peers? Will our children's values come from the current trends in our culture? We think those values should come from us, their parents.

The Coming Crisis

There is a crisis coming. Someday we all face one. A crisis is not merciful to anyone. It challenges adults and children alike. A solid set of family values will allow each of us in our family to make it through the tough times. *Values give us a set of principles to filter our reactions through.* How we react in a crisis as parents will go a long way in determining how our children will react to one when they become adults.

The Coming Temptation

If our kids do not know what is important or what we believe as a family, we are rolling the dice when they are confronted by the temptations of the world. *Values go way beyond a list of dos and don'ts that some parents believe are adequate.*

We cannot set up enough rules to address every decision our kids will encounter. A strong set of family values can address most of the temptations our kids will face. Values provide everyone in the family with a framework for making wise decisions.

The Coming Decisions

Why do some "good" kids go to college and get in trouble?

Our goal should not be to raise perfect children who follow the rules. Our goal should be to raise adults of high character who make wise decisions. Our children will have to make their own decisions when they go to college or just move away from home. So we need to ask ourselves, *Have we taught them how to make wise decisions or just left them with a list of inadequate rules?* Once they leave the house, the decisions our kids make will be up to them. Have we prepared them to make wise decisions?

The Leader's Job in a Family

We are failing in one of our primary responsibilities as a leader if our family does not know what is important to us and what we believe in and why.

There are four steps that anyone leading a family must take to begin seizing that responsibility:

1. Define my family's values

If you are unsure where to start, start with *Courage, Humility, Integrity, Duty, Selflessness,* and *Positivity.* We have provided straightforward and brief definitions for each of these *Habits of Character* throughout the book. As we explain these values to our family, we should ask them questions such as "What does good look like?" and "What do each of these *Habits of Character* look like in action?"

2. Model my family's values

Leaders need to model the behavior that they expect from others. Our families will not follow us if we say something is important and then act contrary to our words. Teenagers know the definition of a *hypocrite.* If they see us as hypocrites, should we be surprised when we lose their respect and they rebel?

3. Over communicate my family's values

No team ever failed because of too much communication but because of too little. A family is the most important team we will ever lead. If we truly believe the *Habits of Character* are important for our family, we must communicate those values at every opportunity. If something is important, it is worth repeating. We cannot expect to impact the actions of the people we are supposed to be leading without the words that influence those actions.

4. Coach my family's values

When family members display *Courage,* we need to encourage them with praise. Conversely, when family members back down from a challenge due to fear, we need to coach them and help them face those fears. As leaders of our families, we are called to coach the generations that follow us to grow into men and women of character. No one else in the world is more responsible for whom our children turn out to be than we, the parents, leading our families.

Character Development

- Our character starts with our ***thoughts***.
- Our thoughts influence our ***words***.
- Our words lead us to our ***actions***.
- Our actions, repeated over time, become our ***habits***.
- Our habits form our ***character***.

The path to developing your character and your family's character starts with your thoughts. What do you believe in? Do you discuss those beliefs to reinforce what good looks like? Do you praise your family when their actions match their words? And do you recognize and reinforce their positive expressions of character as they form the *Habits of Character* we are called to implant in our families?

Leaders of Character Leading *Families of Character*

Leaders of Character believe in their hearts that the character of their family is their top priority and the most lasting legacy we will have on this earth. Wherever our families may have been in the past or may be currently on the character spectrum, the leader of each family is called to take action. We must take action to change, develop, and reinforce our own *Habits of Character* and those of each family member.

Ask any grandparent and they will tell you that leading and developing your children and your children's children are a lifelong mission. As *Leaders of Character* who are called to develop *Families of Character*, we are responsible for diligently teaching the six *Habits of Character* to our children. We need to talk about these habits when we are sitting around the house or having a family meal. We need to identify teachable moments when we walk beside our children or are tucking them in at night. *Courage, Humility, Integrity, Duty, Selflessness,* and *Positivity* need to be the values we wear on our sleeves so our children do not doubt what we stand for. We need to lead in such a way that our house and, more importantly, the behaviors of those who live in it become a billboard for the *Habits of Character* that create *Families of Character*.

Exercises for Developing *Families of Character*: Time to Break a Sweat

The values we hold dear can be identified based on the behaviors we regularly display. What do you display? What do your kids display? Have you done anything to guide your family toward living out a set of values? With these ideas in mind, here are some exercises you can do for and with your family.

Defining

- ✓ Define the values you want your family to stand for. If your kids are old enough (seven years old or above), include them in determining what you stand for.
- ✓ Describe what good looks like. What do *Courage, Humility*, and so on look like in action?
- ✓ Give each family member a value to describe what good looks like.

Modeling

- ✓ Practice the list of exercises that accompanies each chapter in this book. Our families are watching what we do more than they are listening to what we say.

Over Communicating

- ✓ Have weekly family meal discussions on a different *Habit of Character*.
- ✓ Frame your family values and display them prominently.
- ✓ Discuss your values on rides to school or to practices.
- ✓ Use case-study-style discussion to discuss how to make wise decisions when temptations arise. Filter those decisions through your values, not through a list of rules.

Coaching

- ✓ Never miss an opportunity to praise behaviors that exhibit a family member's character.
- ✓ Never miss an opportunity to coach a poor decision by discussing the role of the family's values in how the decision was made.

✓ Refer back to *Courage, Humility, Integrity, Selflessness, Duty,* and *Positivity* when coaching any decision, good or bad.

✓ Discuss the intangible benefits to our character versus the tangible benefits of how people view us, when we stay out of trouble, or receive any rewards or recognition.

Developing Teams of Character

Organizational Character

There is a lot of literature available discussing organizational culture. The culture of a team is the topic of many white papers, articles in business magazines, blogs, and books. Unfortunately, these sources often break down organizational culture by describing dress codes, break rooms, work hours, weekly happy hours, health benefits, pay scales, and the like. While these are nice things to have at work, they are not a true description of an organization's culture. These are the perks. You can have the best perks and benefits in your industry and still work in a poisonous environment.

Those perks and benefits are not the most important things to employees, and they are not why many companies have a problem with employee engagement and subsequently employee turnover. The real issue can be traced back to what we call *Organizational Character*.

Anderson's 12-Word (or Less) Definition of Organizational Character
Our demonstrated values—our habitual behaviors
with our customers and each other

Organizational Character does a better job describing an organization's soul than any list of perks or benefits can do. How we treat, not just others, but also each other, is a true measure of who we are as a team. We can walk into a lot of businesses and be treated like royalty because we are the customer. But when we leave, how do those same people behave with each other? How do they treat each other when no one else is around?

Our habitual behaviors with both our customers and each other are the true measures of the character of a team. Our *Organizational Character* is not who we claim to be. Rather, our *Organizational Character* is best defined by how we behave on a habitual basis.

Knowing What You Stand For

What is important to you? If someone were to ask you what was truly important in your life, what would those things be? Now how would you answer that same question at work? What do you stand for? What do you want your team to stand for?

Knowing what values are important to you and declaring them publicly are the critical first step to ensuring you have the team you want. Values define the behavioral expectations the leader has for her team.

Knowing what we stand for will ensure we will make decisions based on our values, not on our circumstances. Otherwise our decisions will be reactionary and inconsistent. When a leader of a team does not know what she stands for, then that leader's decisions can be unpredictable and inconsistent. This hurts the level of trust others have in their leader.

> *The time to figure out what you stand for is not in the midst of a crisis.*

If *Courage, Humility, Integrity, Selflessness, Duty,* and *Positivity* were your team's values, their responses to tests and challenges would be predictable and would demonstrate high *Organizational Character*. A team's values are the guideposts for making decisions, especially when the tests come.

Do you know what you stand for? Does your team know what you stand for? If the leader does not know what he stands for and if his team members do not know, we should not be surprised when they make choices based on what seems to work at the moment. Without a clear understanding of the team's values and how to filter decisions through those values, pragmatism can lead to the downfall of a team.

A ship left adrift rarely ends up in port.
It almost always ends up on the reef.

Grabbing Hold of the Wheel

Even though they may have the best intentions, many leaders let the *Organizational Character* of their teams just happen. Whether they are leading at work or at home, all the other demands of life overwhelm them. The day-to-day demands of managing—meetings, putting out fires, generating reports, conference calls, etc.—make it hard to focus on the big picture, no matter their best intentions.

The ironic thing is, if we never get past focusing on just staying afloat, our team is truly in danger of ending up on the reef. If a storm comes and they make poor decisions that cause a wreck, who was the person at the helm, steering the ship? We were. The leaders. We leaders need to grab hold of the wheel and steer the ship. Our teams depend on us to know what we stand for and then to guide them through the storms that are bound to come.

A *Leader of Character* can develop a *Team of Character* by following the same character development model we have already presented.

Character Development

- Our character starts with our ***thoughts***.
- Our thoughts influence our ***words***.
- Our words lead us to our ***actions***.
- Our actions, repeated over time, become our ***habits***.
- Our habits form our ***character***.

Once our values are defined by what good looks like (thoughts), then it is time to discuss what good looks like (words).

At this point, you may be thinking, *Stop right there. All of this sounds good, but I don't have time to do any of this at work. I am already overwhelmed with my day-to-day stuff!*

Well, do you have fifteen minutes a week? That's all it takes to lead your team in a discussion related to the values you want them to demonstrate. One company we worked with to define their values came up with the following description of what *Integrity* looks like in action.

Integrity in Action
- We will own our actions and the actions of others on our team.
- We will speak out and always challenge a potential integrity issue.
- We will keep our promises to our clients and to each other.
- We will do the right thing no matter the personal or professional consequences.

Each bullet point could be the foundation for a fifteen-minute discussion about what *Integrity* looks like in action for your team. That time could easily turn out to be the best use of any quarter of an hour in your entire workweek.

Five Steps to Developing *Teams of Character*

The following steps are a summary adapted from The Overwhelmed Manager's Guide to a Winning Culture found online at http://om-guide.com. This is a video-based online course designed to help leaders develop the low-maintenance team of their dreams—a *Team of Character*.

1. Defining your values

What does good look like? What do *Integrity*, *Duty*, or *Selflessness* look like for this team? These will look similar to the *Integrity* example above.

2. Communicating your values

If something is important, it is worth repeating. In fact, it is not the leader's job to communicate the team's values. It is the leader's job to over-communicate those values.

3. Hiring for values

We can't keep hiring people for their competence and then firing them for their character flaws if we want to have *Teams of Character*.

4. Coaching your values

The values a leader claims are not the real standards of a team. Whatever behaviors a leader allows to happen are that leader's real standards.

5. Firing for values

When someone is unwilling to adapt to the values of the team, it is time for a change. To make that change, a leader must believe in the values he claims and have the *Courage* to take action.

For more details, free videos, free values-based interview guides, and access to The Overwhelmed Manager's Guide to a Winning Culture online course, go to http://om-guide.com.

Appendix C
THE 12-WORD (OR LESS) DEFINITIONS

Definition of a Leader of Character

Someone who uses influence to achieve a moral or ethical goal

Definition of Character

Our habitual way of operating: HOW we are is WHO we are!

Definition of Courage

Acting despite perceived or actual risk

Definition of Humility

Believing and acting like "It's not about me"

Definition of Integrity

Doing what is good, right, and proper, even at personal cost

Definition of Selflessness

Putting the needs of others before my own needs, desires, or convenience

Definition of Duty

Taking action based on our assigned tasks and moral obligations

Definition of Positivity

Displaying a positive and/or can-do attitude in all circumstances

Appendix D

RESOURCES

Here are some resources we highly recommend:

Leaders of Character Online Resources
My Mirror Character Assessment at alslead.com/character-test
Anderson Leadership Solutions website: http://alslead.com/character-test or http://alslead.com.

- Exclusive membership group for continually updated character-building materials for you, your teams, and your family.
- Also includes information on booking for speaking engagements.
- Includes blogs, podcasts, and videos. Register to get regular updates via email.
- More *Leader of Character* resources will be added consistently to include:
  ◊ Books
  ◊ Workbooks
  ◊ Audiobooks
  ◊ Video libraries

The Overwhelmed Manager's Guide to a Winning Culture Website:
http://overwhelmedmanagersguide.com or http://om-guide.com.

- Free OMG Power Pack in PDF. Includes:
  ◊ Vision and Mission Statement Development Template
  ◊ Values Statements Examples
  ◊ Values-Based Interview Guide
- Free Training Videos
  ◊ Winning Culture Vision
  ◊ Hiring for Values
  ◊ What Good Looks Like
- Plus The Overwhelmed Mangers Guide to a Winning Culture Online Course
  ◊ Six video-based modules
  ◊ Multiple additional downloadable resources

Acknowledgments

A book like this would not have been possible without the wisdom and support of a large number of people. So many people have influenced our thoughts and beliefs on leadership that it is hard to acknowledge them all. But here is our humble attempt to give credit where credit is due.

We would like to thank the men and women who taught us so much at the United States Military Academy at West Point. These people are the best our nation has to offer, and they are dedicated to building young cadets into *Leaders of Character*. We thank all of you for your dedication to our development.

To our classmates from the West Point graduate classes of 1956 and 1988: The class of 1956 served our country through Vietnam and the Cold War, and one graduate commanded our forces in Operation Desert Storm. They became business leaders who shaped our country through the last three decades and continue to impact our society into their retirement years. The class of 1988 has been deployed more and spent more years in a combat environment than almost any West Point class in history. The leaders who are now off the battlefield are the standard bearers for leading with character in our current culture. You inspire us. We are honored to be counted among you.

To those we had the privilege to serve beside and were blessed to lead: You might have gotten the raw end of the deal by being at the receiving end of our mistakes that helped us to formulate the lessons in this book. We thank you for your patience with us, your grace, your friendship, and your loyalty through the years we worked together. We are better because we got the opportunity to work with you.

To the greats leaders and thinkers whose shoulders we stand upon: People like Ken Blanchard, John Maxwell, Steven Covey, Patrick Lencioni, Henry Cloud, Dave Ramsey, Dan Miller, and others have led the charge for developing leaders. We acknowledge your previous work and its influence on our book. We are not competing with any of you by writing this book. We are joining you in trying to make a difference and in impacting our world through our words.

We also want to specifically thank Dr. Joey Faucette who spoke truth to Dave. When Dave said he wished he could write a book with *The General,* Joey said, "What are you waiting for?" It was the kick in the behind Dave needed and the catalyst that got us to this point.

In the first stages of this process Dave's intern from a local university created the first version of the book cover that is very similar to what you see today. He also created the graphics you see inside this book. We thank Skyler Hefley for his dedicated work. To prospective employers -Skyler would be a great hire if you are looking! Contact Dave if you ever want to know about Skyler.

To the professionals who believed in our work and helped make it better: Working with the professionals at Morgan James Publishing has been an honor. Karen Anderson, our Acquisition Editor, became an outspoken advocate for our work. She is the one who got us noticed. David Hancock, Founder of Morgan James Publishing, was personally involved in the details of developing this book and planning for its success. Megan Malone, our Managing Editor, and the marketing professionals at Morgan James spent a lot of time answering questions from two neophyte authors. Finally, we want to thank Bill Watkins who was a great editor to work with and who improved our work with both skill and eloquence. We thank you all.

To our friends and families: Thank you for your encouragement and slogging through the early versions of our book when our ideas were not polished. Your time and interest in our success was truly a humbling act of service to us.

From Dave: I want to specifically acknowledge my father, aka *The General,* for the lifetime of modeling and mentoring he has given me. I may have strayed from the path at times, but your patience and belief in me ultimately made me want to make you as proud of me as I am of you.

Thank you to my mother Joyce, who always believed in me and set the example for me when it came to loving others and living a life of caring and compassion.

I also want to thank my wife Elizabeth who encouraged me to write a book and has been my biggest cheerleader as I have finally gotten it done. She is the best thing in my world, has given me a great family, and is my best friend.

From Jim: Although in this book I am referred to as *The General*, I did not begin my life thinking that I was going to be leading soldiers in combat and later working with business executives to help them understand what it takes to become *Leaders of Character*. You see, I was raised in a county orphanage in New Lexington, Ohio. It was Josie and Rufus Dornbirer who led me early in life to understand why my character was how people would judge me. They were the ones who taught me that my character would come to me through my faith in our Lord and Savior.

Finally, we both want to acknowledge the Lord our God. Lord, if there is anything in this book that is not what you would want, we pray it falls on deaf ears. Thank you for giving us this opportunity.

ABOUT THE AUTHORS

General James L. Anderson (*The General*)

General Jim Anderson grew up in a county orphanage in Ohio after his mother died and his father abandoned him and his siblings. Though an excellent student and the quarterback of his high school football team, he realized that the only way to afford college was through one of the military academies. He was accepted to West Point and graduated with the class of 1956. He was an infantry officer, an Army Ranger School instructor, and a veteran of two tours in combat in Vietnam. He earned a Silver Star, two Bronze Stars for Valor, and a Purple Heart while leading soldiers in combat.

The General spent a total of forty-one years leading soldiers in the United States Army. His final twenty-four years were spent back at West Point where he held the title of Master of the Sword as the Head of the Physical Education

Department. *The General* spent his final twenty-four years of service devoted to developing our nation's future Army officer corps.

Now retired, General James L. Anderson has almost twenty years developing and training *Leaders of Character* as a consultant and speaker for over one hundred Fortune 500 companies and multiple federal agencies.

He has been married to his high school sweetheart, Joyce, for close to sixty years and is the father to his daughter Terri and his son and co-author David. He is also the proud grandfather of Jake and Samantha.

You can learn more about *The General* at: alslead.com/aboutmydad

Dave Anderson (*The Business Guy*)

Dave Anderson grew up in a stable home thanks to the love of his father (above) and mother. He graduated from West Point with the class of 1988. He was a field artillery officer serving as a forward observer during Operation Desert Storm. He earned a Bronze Star while leading soldiers in combat.

The Business Guy left the Army and joined a Fortune 50 company where he spent twenty years in sales and various sales leadership positions, achieving significant awards and recognition as an individual and a leader of teams. He now owns Anderson Leadership Solutions where he takes his passion for developing *Leaders of Character* to new heights as a speaker, talk-radio-show host, blogger, and consultant.

Dave has been married to Elizabeth for over twenty years and is the proud father of his twins, Jake and Samantha.

You can learn more about Dave at his website: alslead.com/aboutme

CONNECT WITH US

We enjoy hearing from our readers online. Below are some places you can find us. Make sure to mention you read our book, *Becoming a Leader of Character!*

Website/Blog/Speaking
http://andersonleadershipsolutions.com

LinkedIn
https://www.linkedin.com/in/daveanderson1988

Facebook
https://www.facebook.com/alslead

Twitter
https://twitter.com/daveanderson88 or @daveanderson88

Email
info@alslead.com